Thru His Eyes:
The Military Life of Brutha Sylvester Bracey, Sr. Vietnam Recon Vet

Markus Bracey

Copyright © 2021 Markus Bracey

All rights reserved.

ISBN: 9798514742530

DEDICATION

This book was dedicated to all of us war veterans. Thank you for your service.

TABLE OF CONTENTS

ACKNOWLEDGMENTS I
INTRODUCTION 1
    Setting the Stage 4
    Why Now? 5
FIRST TOUR IN VIETNAM 1967-1968 8
CHAPTER 1 9
    THE DANANG AIRPORT ATTACK 9
CHAPTER 2 11
    CON THIEN NOVEMBER 1967 11
CHAPTER 3 17
    LET GO IN THE AMBUSH! 17
CHAPTER 4 21
    AMBUSH ON HIGHWAY 9 BY HILL 881 21
CHAPTER 5 33
    BATTLE OF DONG HA OR DAI DO 33
INTERMISSION 43
THE SECOND TOUR 44
CHAPTER 6 45
    ASHAU VALLEY THE WALKING DEAD 1968-1969 45
CHAPTER 7 53
    JOINING THE SOG 53
CHAPTER 8 67
    THE SEARCH FOR PEACE 67

CHAPTER 9	79
FINAL SUMMARY	79
SYLVESTER WORE A COAT OF MANY COLORS	84
CHAPTER 10	87
LET'S GET PERSONAL	87
Out of Body Experience	89
REFERENCES	95
ABOUT THE AUTHOR	97

ACKNOWLEDGMENTS

I want to say thank you to all of the people who made this book possible by supporting me and believing in me. I want to thank Pops for trusting me to tell the stories the way he told them to me. I want to thank my mom, Angella Allen and my aunt, Celeste Trussell for helping me bring this book to life by typing it up and doing all the things I hate. My Aunt Celeste also gave me the title of the book. These women have been my rock throughout! I love you Mom and Auntie!

Special thanks to my publisher Dr. Veronica Walters. She wrapped it up, smoothed out the rough edges and put a ribbon on it. I would also like to give special thanks to all of the Vietnam War veterans who made this book possible through their blood, sweat and tears. 0

Thank you to Spike Lee for doing the movie Da Five Bloods that shed some light on the presence and experience of Black men in Vietnam. Huge thanks to D. L. Hugely for sharing the video from the documentary on Black G.I.s which featured Pops. It was our first time seeing the video. Man, if you hadn't shared it, we might not have ever seen it. Thank you to all of the Youtubers who created content around Pops conversation about racism in the military and the war whether it was sharing him speaking or creating music around it. Thanks for helping to make Pops visible.

I'd also like to thank my family for the moral, mental and physical support. Last, but not least, I'd like to thank you, the Reader, the audience. Thank you for having an open mind. I forgot, one more. I'd like to thank the Academy Awards of Books (LOL) before I get my award! Is he being serious? Yes, I am!

INTRODUCTION

My pops was known for being for the people, about the people, and loving the people. Hello readers and thank you for your energy of reception. I am honored to share with you the stories my pops shared about the Vietnam War or the War as it's known. The fact that you are here means that you are in for a treat.

Let me introduce myself. My name is Markus Bracey. I am a United States Gulf War Army Veteran. I served in the Navy as well. I am legally the first son of Sylvester Bracey, Sr., Marine Recon/SOG (Special Operation Group) Vietnam War veteran from 1967 to 1969. My Pops shared his experiences of the War with me and my brother, Sylvester Bracey, Jr. Before I get started, let me be the first to say that I am not a professional writer. This was my first book, and I will be sharing these stories and experiences from a narrator's perspective. Also, let me just say I was not in the Vietnam War. I am only sharing stories and experiences from my pops' point of view -- through his eyes. If I do my job right, you will feel me and feel Pops' stories almost as if you were there when my pops told me the stories. This book will not be written like your traditional book and will be more of a father, who was a veteran, sitting down and telling his stories to a son who was also a veteran. That was it – we are simply veterans, not writers.

As kids, my pops had us doing the Black Power handshake, marching in circles, singing the Marine Anthem, and telling us these amazing stories about what happened in the War from his perspective. Just to pique your interest, have you ever heard of a Vietnam veteran who was caught by the enemy, not once, but twice and never shot or taken POW (Prisoner of War)? I know this sounds interesting, but interesting was an understatement. Once you read this book, you will agree. My Pops stuck to his proud Marine oath and never shared his stories with the public but now you will be able to hear those stories as he told them.

In Pops' second tour, he was asked if he would like to join a secret operation with no more Reconnaissance (Recon) in Vietnam. Pops had to sign a contract stating that he would never talk. He never talked about this secret operation for over 20 years. Pops signed the contract and joined the SOG Team. SOG means Studies and Observation Group.

Unfortunately, my dad left this world on December 7, 2019. Rest in Peace/Power (RIP) Sylvester Bracey, Sr. I felt that it was my duty as a son and as a veteran to put his story out there. I did get permission from Pops in his last years of life to do just that. My only regret was that we had planned for me to go to St. Louis (*where he lived at the time of his death*) and videotape him talking about the War. I didn't get the chance to go. However, I did reaffirm the stories that I've heard over the years. Pops gave me the greenlight to share these stories saying, "Marrk, you got it. Now let the people know. They need to know how it really was in The Nam." So that's exactly what I am doing now.

There are a few things that are different about my pops' Vietnam stories. For instance, in this book, you will see a timeline of events happening in the War through both tours making it easier for you to fact check. Another difference was that you are hearing or reading these stories from a Recon Marine's perspective. That was a totally different perspective from those on the military base. Another difference was the Black perspective regarding racism. There was racism that was going on in America during the War; racism *in* the War, as well as racism we imposed on the Vietnamese People. All these challenges made Pops' story exceptional. Plus, my pops was caught twice by the enemy and lived to tell these amazing stories. I remind you these stories came from an 18–19-year-old Marine Veteran, my dad, Sylvester Bracey, Sr. in South Vietnam.

I promise you, if Pops told me ten battles, I researched them. I went to Google, YouTube, Military Times, etc. and I took quotes and things Pops said with times and incidents that happened in the War and listened to other Marines saying the same thing with some of the same stories with video footage. I was like, "OH, MY GOD; Pops' stories are really true." If I looked at ten of Pops stories, I instantly connected with seven stories exactly like Pops said. The other three stories, I could not find because these stories were too bullet-hot for cameras. Examples, like Hill 881, being overrun by the enemy NVA (North Vietnamese Army). When it was that hot, there are no cameras. It's you live or you die. You are just ducking bullets and shooting back. Stay down, hug the ground! Let me paint this picture a little better. My Pops had all the stories that you may see on Google and YouTube from the military base perspective, but that was a totally different perspective from a Marine Recon Team.

The Recon teams saw ten times more of the enemies' actions than those that were on the military base. Being in Recon, to those non-military people, was like a group of Rambos. A five-to-seven-man fire team that was dropped off by helicopters or planes in enemy territories. The Recon team's job was to hide amongst the enemy, watch the enemy's actions, report all actions and locations; and most importantly, JUST DON'T GET CAUGHT! Recon teams also call-in airstrikes and artillery while they are among the enemies. Last, they call in for extraction from the enemy's area usually ending up in a hot Landing Zone (which means the enemy was shooting at the helicopter while trying to pick up the Recon team). My point was the Recon team saw ten times more of the enemy than the bases saw. So, the stories you are getting and reading now are coming from Pops doing Recon and when they attacked our bases.

Whether or not these stories are different from your average Vietnam Vet, I will let you be the judge. You, the Reader, will see in this book a slow escalation from Pops' entry point into the War with a timeline so the stories do not lose you. You will also see from Pops' perspective the War goes from worse to worser to the worst. You will be surprised to have a pleasant, crazy ending that you probably never would have imagined.

Have you ever wondered what really happened in Vietnam? The War carries so much mystique and Vets act crazy sometimes like it was something unexplainable. I would like to welcome you to the Vietnam War from a Recon perspective from Sylvester Bracey, Sr., Marine Recon/SOG 1967-1968, and 1968-1969.

You are about to enter another world. I will do my best to remember, describe, and tell you stories as my pops told them to me all my life. Once again, I am not a book writer. I am just a veteran sharing detailed stories of events that happened in his two tours in Vietnam.

Setting the Stage

In this section of the introduction, I am going to set the stage for you with battle location and other background information from the war to help orient you for the stories that you are about to read. Also, you will see pictures of Pops in the War as well as his personal Recon maps in Vietnam and articles he sent home from Vietnam in this book. To begin here was a list of places that my pops mentioned during his service in Vietnam. Pops either performed recon, visited the bases, was at these bases, had small firefights or had big battles at all of these places. You will see these locations mentioned throughout the book including Danang, Con Thien, Gio Lingh, The Rock Pile, Camp Carroll, Camp Evans, Dongha or Di Do, Cua Viet, The Country of Laos, Recon for SOG on the Ho Chi Mingh Trail, Ashau Valley, Hill 881s, 861 881n, Khe Sanh, Cam lo, and Calu. These are all the places Pops has mentioned to me that he was at in the war for different reasons. All of his action was on the frontline. To help you understand Pops' perspectives in the stories, you have to understand the difference between a regular troop and a Recon platoon.

RIFs (Recon In Force) can be detached and attached to any units in the war needing reconnaissance. Before any mass units went out on patrols, the area was reconned first. Pops could be doing recon for literally any units close by needing recon. Like the 82nd Airborne Army Unit in the Walking Dead. They needed recon before they went into the Ashau Valley. So, my pops was not Army 82nd Airborne but doing recon he was there for the Walking Dead and Hamburger Hill as well. I am trying to get you to understand that Recon teams were not stationary. They were in all or a lot of battles even from other units and operations especially when we were doing the attacking. Everywhere we were about to attack on foot was reconned first. Simply put, the Recon teams would go to any area sometimes with dogs. If the dog caught the scent of the enemy presence at that time, the Recon team would fall back or come back to our troops giving them the green light to go forward. Recon let them know that the enemy was up there. Lot of times, the enemy would let the Recon team pass through with no incident or ambushes just to get to our troops in mass. But there were other times that the Recon team just got ambushed or demolished. Recon teams were used as bait to attract the enemy to come out and attack us. But let me slow down a minute because I'm telling "too much" because this was just the introduction.

Why Now?

You may be asking yourself what made me write this book…Now? The answer to that question alone was something incredible that I wasn't expecting but it has lit a fire in me to make sure that my pops' story was told. So, let me break it down for you.

As I said, Pops passed December 7, 2019. Pops and I had already talked about sharing his stories for years. In August 2020, we got a call from his widow/wife, Bridgett. She told us to go to D. L. Hughley's page on Facebook because they had a video of our dad in Vietnam speaking on racism in the war. I was like, what??? D. L. Hughley's page? I instantly went on Facebook and saw my pops in a 1969 video in a mess hall leading Marines talking about racism in the war. Google or YouTube, Sylvester Bracey Marine, racism, or discrimination in Vietnam 1970 and Pops' video should pop up. Pops' video went viral with over 6 million views which was amazing. But I want to give a special thanks to Spike Lee. If Spike Lee had never made the movie *"Da 5 Bloods,"* then my pops' video might not have ever surfaced. Spike Lee made his movie based on one of the old documentaries of racism in the Vietnam War from 1969-1970. My Pops' character was not in the movie, *Da 5 Bloods*. But someone saw that original documentary and saw Pops' part for the Marines and shared it. After the video went viral and was viewed 6 Million times, I was able to simply match his video with his war stories in this book. I just want you to know and understand the person that you are reading about.

I want you to know that even the existence of this video footage was another story that my brother and I heard while we were under 10 years of age. Pops said, "Didn't your Momma show you all me on tv talking about racism in the war?" We both laughed, and said, "Naw, Mama didn't show us no videos of you on TV talking in the war." My Pops was a humble man, so he never spoke about it after that time. In Pops' head, they didn't see the video, so okay! There was no sense in bringing it up again. The fact was that Pops also never saw his video. It was as if the cameraman in the war had lied to them. They were thinking the people at home would see this video. The actual truth was that it did come on TV in a 1970 documentary. My mom just did not know about it or see it. Pops did not know all this time that his video had been stored in the Smithsonian Black History Museum. Pops made the Black History books at 19 years old, but never knew it.

So, when I saw D. L. Hughley's post about my dad on Facebook, I got on the post to represent the family. I noticed they did not even know my pops name all these years. When I got on the post, there were 15 thousand shares and 10 thousand comments on that one post. My nephew, Sylvester Bracey, III shared the same post to Twitter. On Twitter, he was at 20 thousand shares and 15 thousand comments. Of course, the saddest part was that I wish Pops could have seen all of the support he's getting now. Unfortunately, he passed December 7, 2019 so he just missed this recognition. RIP Pops! The comments on the posts were awesome. The people loved my pops. My brother, Sylvester Bracey, Jr. and nephew, Sylvester Bracey, III responded to calls for interviews from history networks, YouTube channels, even Channel 7 News came out and interviewed them. I watched the interviews of my brother and they talked about the racism in the war and Pops' views towards racism. As a Gulf War Veteran, I noticed they really did not talk about Pops' experiences in the war much besides the racism. The thing was that it was Pops' war experiences that hardened his stance and views towards Racism. I truly felt that Pops' interview on racism could not encompass my pops' total Vietnam war experience. So, I am grabbing the torch as an older brother and son of my father and moving forward with his war experiences. My Pops told me *"Let the people know."*

I lived with my pops 10 years more than my brother in our adult lives in different places and cities. So naturally I got more of the stories from the war. I got Pops' permission before death to share with you. Now when you hear these war stories and Pops fighting for America, you will see why Pops was not accepting racism on the bases. *"We are all Marines, same team!"* was Pops' point of view which was why I am compelled to write this book now!

Let's Get Started!
Welcome to the Jungle 1967, 1968-1969

First Tour in Vietnam 1967-1968

CHAPTER 1

THE DANANG AIRPORT ATTACK

My Pops was drafted into the Vietnam War at approximately 18 years of age. Pops went to basic training and Advanced Individual Training at Paris Island Marine Base in the summer of 1967. By the fall of 1967, Pops was in Vietnam. Pops said when he got there, the first thing he noticed was the HEAT. He said that it was over 100 degrees every day. Pops also noticed a different type of smell. He said it was unexplainable, but not pleasant at all. He was at Danang Airport which was his entry point into the War. He stayed in Danang for maybe a month getting oriented to the Marine Vietnam war life. He was a Proud Marine. Let me give you a little background about Vietnam terrain. Pops said it was a very beautiful country. All colors and hues were so vivid. The blues were bluer, and the greens were greener. Pops said they had beautiful pretty skies, but it was always wet. It rained half of the year. Most of the time, Pops was on the front line in the jungle. It was very mountainous and hilly. There was ten-foot elephant grass and usually 6 inches to 2 feet of water on the ground half of the time. Yes, this was the jungle. There were no hippos, but there were tigers, monkeys, snakes, and elephants that lived and roamed freely.

Let's get back to the War. Pops mentioned there was one big attack in the Fall of 1967. The Danang Airport Attack. For your own personal reference, you can YouTube the Vietnam Danang Airport Attack. The Vietcong soldiers attacked the Marine's headquarters at Danang. The Vietcong were the people of Vietnam helping the war against America's intrusions. The NVA were the North Vietnamese Army. We were fighting different groups. America really did not know with the Vietcong which ones were enemies and which ones were innocent civilians. In the attack, some Vietcong soldiers mortar attacked the base. These attacks at the 1967 Danang airport resulted in plenty of dead and wounded marines. This attack was Pops' first taste of the Vietnam War, but it definitely wasn't his last.

Chapter 2

Con Thien November 1967

Pops' first mission or assignment came approximately, November Fall of 1967. Pops was sent to Con Thien on the DMZ front line. DMZ was the demilitarized zone, a 5-mile neutral or no fighting zone between the nations at war. Con Thien was the last border town before entering North Vietnam. In other words, after a month in Vietnam, Pops was sent to the front line. Question, why was America even in the Vietnam War? Vietnam never attacked America. Absolutely, that was a Great Point! Potuses Kennedy, Johnson and Nixon were all presidents during this long war. Simply put, you've got North Vietnam and South Vietnam. North Vietnam was working with China and Russia and was considered to be communist. America feared North Vietnam would turn South Vietnam communist as well as neighboring countries, Laos, Cambodia, and Thailand. America was trying to prevent a communist region so to assist the South Vietnamese government, we attacked North Vietnam.

Now that we have some background, let's get back to Con Thien. Pops said Con Thien was a muddy bloodbath for marines. He said it was so muddy, you could take a step and go down 12 inches in mud every step. It was very hard to run in mud under attack. Pops said the North Vietnamese Army could attack Con Thien routinely with mortars and long-range artillery. The North Vietnamese Army used Russian long-range artillery that shot further than United States long-range artillery meaning they could shoot and hit us, but we could not reach them. We were a sitting target that could not shoot back unless we were close. The US soldiers just got bombed in the mud. Pops said all we did at Con Thien was run for cover or to the bunkers. He really did not like Con Thien because we could not fight back. The North Vietnamese Army were too far out of range to be attacked. So whenever Pops talked about this battle, he mentioned lots of casualties. He only stayed at Con Thien for a few weeks. His next marine mission was the Hills of the demilitarized zone guarding our base at Khe Sanh.

On United States bases in the hills of the jungles of Vietnam, Pops did Recon missions around Hill 861, Hill 881s, and Hill 881n. Also, I have included a picture of my pops' actual Recon map used in the war [Exhibit A]. You can see pictures of an article in Stars and Stripes magazine in Vietnam that Pops sent home to my mom describing the setup around Khe Sanh Base [Exhibit B].

Also, to not alienate you the Reader from the stories, I encourage you to go to YouTube to verify the stories and feel the impact. For instance, on YouTube search for Con Thien Base Attack Fall 1967, the Hill fights Vietnam, or Hill 881 January 1968. Although you will have your mental pictures just reading, being able to see the actual attacks and hearing other soldiers saying the exact same things helps to support the stories and give an even more complete picture of what happened.

THRU HIS EYES

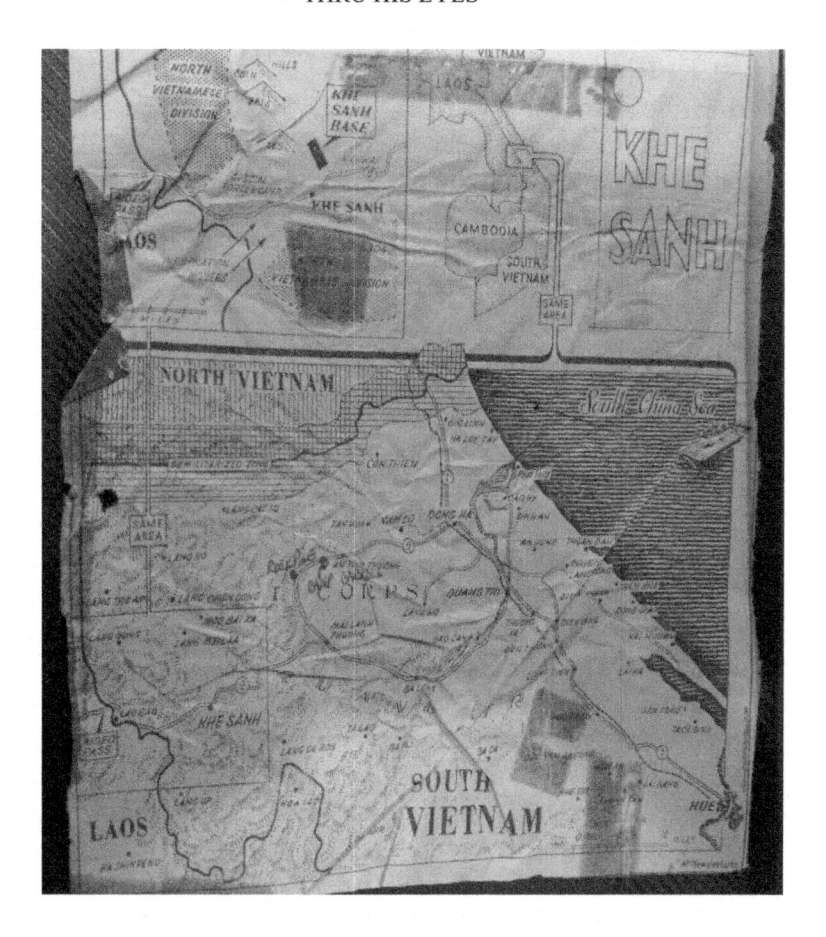

Exhibit A. This is a copy of the Recon Map that was actually sent home by Pops.

I told you earlier that I had included my pops' Recon map from the war, but I want to define Recon. What was Recon? Recon was a secret covert reconnaissance mission that usually consisted of a 5-to-9-man assault team like a group of Rambos. The team was flown in by helicopter and plane and dropped off alone in enemy territory. Their job was to find the enemy, report all movements, actions, personnel, and location without being detected. They eventually could call in airstrikes, artillery or troops if needed. Doing recon was a very dangerous job. The hardest part was just not getting caught.

Marine infantry battalions did not have Recon. Marines had Recon platoons. These Recon teams were attached to any U.S. Infantry units needing recon before they went out on any preplanned attack. Pops spoke many times that it was a hot LZ or hot landing zone for entry or exit. The enemy was everywhere shooting at the troops landing or being extracted from the jungle. My point in emphasizing Recon was that Pops got the "Bird Eye View" of the War. For example, Pops sent home the article about Khe Sanh to my mom approximately December 1967. Pops also let my mom know, at this time, he was around the Khe Sanh base. In the article, it said the North Vietnamese Army (NVA) were secretly building up troops around the Khe Sanh base estimated at 20,000 troops. I remind you we had maybe ten small fire bases along the front line, maybe 500 troops per base. We had one big mass troop base in Khe Sanh with 5,000 marines. The actual battle at Khe Sanh did not start until late January 1968. The North Vietnamese were actually still building up their forces. However, the U.S. bases could not see their efforts, but the Recon team saw all of that. Mass enemy troops were on the move. Pops said he knew it was going to be something big because of the number of troops and amount of ammo and artillery he saw while he was watching the enemy during Recon. Another reminder, up until that point, Pops was mainly fighting the Vietcong in small firefights and not the North Vietnamese Army. It was totally different, although they were on the same team. The Vietcong were like me and you, grabbing a rifle out of the closet and fighting for America. The North Vietnamese Army was like the Army, Navy, Airforce, and Marines for real.

Let's recap the timeline. Pops entered basic training in the Summer 1967. He was in Vietnam Fall 1967. He experienced the Danang Airport Attack Fall 1967 and Bloody Con Thien Attack November, December 1967. Now I want you to buckle up because we are just getting started.

Pops said that we, the United States forces, owned the day. The North Vietnamese Army and Vietcong owned the nights. Once again, it was hard for U.S. troops to know whether people were Vietcong or innocent Vietnamese. Pops mentioned one time that a Vietnamese kid gave a U.S. soldier an apple. The soldier bit it and it had a razor in it. They had to shoot the kid. Pops also said it was common for G.I.'s to get STD's from the Vietnamese hookers that hung around our bases. Lots of times, the women would also have razors in their vaginas. These are things that are difficult for those without military experience to imagine. And it was made more difficult because we did not know who the enemy Vietcong was which created a lot of uncertainty and risk on the part of our military. In fact, one time a Vietnamese barber for the base ended up in the wire in the morning. He was a Vietcong. A famous saying over there was "Gooks in the wire. Gooks in the wire." Pops said you just didn't know who was who! But that was just one of Pops' encounters. Let's go on to Pops' next encounter.

Chapter 3

LET GO IN THE AMBUSH!

Let's get back to Pops' journey in the Hills of Vietnam, Mid-January 1968. Pops went on a parts run to Cam Lo or Calu. I cannot remember which one. But what I do know was that whichever one it was, Pops' story surrounding that parts run will allow you to get a new appreciation for what happened in Vietnam. Check it out.

Pops' main job was doing Recon, but when he was not doing Recon, his second job was generator operator. The base was on top of the Hill and needed generator power to operate the base. Pops was responsible for making sure the base had power. Pops would operate the generator in the morning, chill all day, and operate the generator at night. It was mandatory for Pops to turn on the lights at night. On this day, he turned on the generator, and hung out for a while on the base. Some Marines were making a routine run for parts to Cam Lo. Cam Lo was only 20 miles away. Pops jumped on the truck and took the ride just to kill some time. He didn't even grab his weapon. Just a routine ride to Cam Lo was 20 minutes there to get parts and 20 minutes to get back. They rode down Highway 9, made it to Cam Lo and got the parts. On the way back five minutes from the Hill base, there was a fork in the road for Highway 9. One road led to the base up the hill, the other road led to the neighboring country Laos five miles the other way. They were ambushed at the fork in the road only five minutes from the base. The Marines jumped out their trucks and started defending against the ambush. Pops said from the barrage of fire power they received, "these ain't Vietcong." They had to call for Airstrikes and artillery from the base on top of the Hill.

Pops said, "These are North Vietnamese Army troops en masse." Pops was kind of puzzled because these North Vietnamese Army troops were in mass so close to the base. I remind you again that Pops had mostly been fighting Vietcong troops and not the North Vietnamese Army whenever they stayed to fight. This was different and do not forget Pops did not bring his weapon, so he assisted the Marine with the 50 caliber machine gun.

It did not take long for Pops to realize it was almost evening and Pops must get back to the base on the Hill. He had to turn on the generator for power and light through the night for the base or this could get much worse. After maybe a half hour of experiencing the North Vietnamese Army ambush, Pops made the decision to walk to the base up the hill -- alone with no weapon. Remember this was the fork in the road. One side led to the base, only minutes away by vehicle, the other side led to the country Laos and this was where the enemy were known to attack and come from. The first time Pops told me and my brother this story we had to be maybe 8 or 9 years old. What happens next…OMG!

I knew there was something special about Pops and in my head, he was a Superhero. When Pops told this story to my brother and I, I could never forget this. Pops said because the ambush came from the Laos side of the fork in the road, he started walking the other direction towards the base in the jungle up the hill. Listen closely, Reader. Pops said he had to walk about a mile or so up this hill, by himself with NO WEAPON. The ambushed Marines were still fighting heavily as he walked up the hill to save the base. I will never forget his energy telling us this story.

The base was on top of Hill 881 and Pops was not supposed to be gone off the base. The only way they would know was if the base lights did not come on, or if they had no night power because of him leaving for the parts run. Pops described that death walk up the hill as he listened to the heavy fire power and the ambushed Marines in the background. He could hear and see our artillery assisting the Marines shooting from the top of the hill, the base. Pops said he was thinking to himself, there had to be at least three or four companies of North Vietnamese Army soldiers attacking the ambushed Marines. Pops said that it was maybe ten or twelve Marines in a few trucks. So, yes, they were outnumbered, but usually artillery or airstrikes would even out the battle. The same way Pops underestimated the enemy by not grabbing his weapon was the same way Pops underestimated the number of North Vietnamese Army soldiers engaging in the ambush against the Marines.

As he walked up the hill listening to the fight, he was really concerned. Like, how many was it really? Pops' words verbatim were, "As I walked up the hill, Marrk, I could feel 'em all around me. Marrk, I knew I had eyes on me. My senses told me the NVAs are all around me and I am walking up this hill with no weapon. Marrk, I don't know why, but for some reason, they didn't shoot."

Sylvester Bracey, Sr.

CHAPTER 4

AMBUSH ON HIGHWAY 9 BY HILL 881

Pops said, "I know one thing for sure, they are here, and they got eyes on me. I feel 'em. Marrk, I could feel them watching me go up this hill. It took about 30 minutes or more, but I made it to the top of Hill 881, the base. Thank God. I turned on the lights and power like normal before nightfall. I explained to the proper authorities the ambush, as the base artillery shelled that area heavy all night." I remind you; U.S. troops owned the day, and the North Vietnamese Army and Vietcong owned the night. With that being said, we were not sending out troops to help fight until daybreak... early morning. Pops said you could hear the fighting all night. By early morning, two or three Marines finally followed Pops' lead and walked back to the base. All of them were badly wounded. The other Marines in the ambush were either wounded too badly to walk back to the base or KIA (Killed in Action- Dead).

A couple of days later, Pops was called for a Recon patrol on January 19, 1968. Just so, you know, this was the Recon patrol that spotted the enemy en masse that started The Battle of Khe-Sanh 77-day siege. On this Recon patrol very close to the Hills base, his Recon team was ambushed by the North Vietnamese Army. Pops said the barrage of firepower was so heavy like five Recon Marines versus hundreds of North Vietnamese Army. With this overwhelming firepower from the North Vietnamese Army, the Recon team instantly retreated. Remember the Recon team's job was not to fight the battle but to make contact calls in artillery, airstrikes or call for troops as they fell back to the company. Pops said the North Vietnamese Army was deep. They were everywhere. Just for the Readers' visual, you can search on YouTube for The Battle of Khe Sanh, Colonel Lownds. You will see that it started with the January 19th Recon patrol. The Recon team came back to the top of the Hill, the base, and reported that they think it was a battalion of North Vietnamese Army soldiers. Hey, Readers, they were underestimating again.

On January 20, 1968, the Marines sent out two companies of Marines at first daylight for this search and destroy mission. Pops said, "Marrk, they fought all day... heavy fighting even with the base shooting artillery mortars and calling in air strikes." Pops said it sounded like a thousand guns, bombs, and artillery going off at the same time all day long. He said by nighttime, they came back. He said not many made it back. Pops said, "We sent out two companies of Marines, that was a couple of hundred Marines. There were under 20 Marines that made it back, almost all wounded or shot." Hey Reader, this was Vietnam. You are still just getting a taste of the War.

So, the base called for reinforcements, but by now, the North Vietnamese Army had cut off and stopped all traffic on Highway 9. Meaning they are cut off and can only be airlifted or resupplied by air. The bottom line, Hill 881, was cut off and totally surrounded by North Vietnamese Army troops en masse. The base prepared to send out a couple more companies of Marines in the morning. Unfortunately, the North Vietnamese Army had plans too. The North Vietnamese Army attacked. On January 21, 1968 at about 3:00 a.m., the North Vietnamese Army unleashed and attacked the base on top of Hill 881 in full force. Let us go back. Remember, days earlier, Pops walked up this hill. Pops said he felt them watching him go up the hill. Pops didn't know they had tunneled positions in the middle of the hill. The only reason they did not shoot Pops was because they would have given away their position. When Pops walked up the hill, they were still building and getting in place for this attack. These are the same 20,000 to 40,000 North Vietnamese Army troops Pops could see doing Recon in the Hills that were trying to surround the Khe Sanh base and our 5,000 Marines. Simultaneously, as they attacked Hill 881, the North Vietnamese Army also attacked Khe Sanh base. This was the start of The Battle of Khe Sanh, but Pops was too occupied with this Hill fight.

Pops said for him, this was the first time the North Vietnamese Army attacked our base in force. From Pops' perspective, all before this, the North Vietnamese Army was still preparing for this battle not fighting but allowing the Vietcong to fight us as the North Vietnamese Army just supported the Vietcong. He said they hit the base ammo dump first so there were rounds and ammunition going off everywhere on the Hill base. Plus, the shooting from the North Vietnamese Army and the Marines, it was Hell on Earth. Pops said every hour or so the North Vietnamese Army was sending 150-man waves up the hill. It was non-stop fight or die on Hill 881. Marines called for support from other units on other hills. They also called in air support for attack, medevacs for the wounded, and air support for much needed supplies, food, water, and ammo. Pops said the North Vietnamese Army kept shooting down the support helicopters. Finally, the Marines from other hills made it to the bottom of Hill 881 on foot. I've got to give you the visual. I know your mind was painting the picture but search on YouTube, William Dabney, slaughtered marines. So now, we have a couple of companies of Marines under attack on the base on top of the Hill. The Marines on the bottom of the Hill were ambushed and attacked by a massive circle of different North Vietnamese Army surrounding the whole hill. The North Vietnamese Army forced the bottom Marines up the Hill to the other North Vietnamese Army entrenched in the middle of the Hill. Yeah, the ones that didn't shoot Pops taking that hill death walk days earlier. The combination attack slaughtered all the Marines trying to help support the Marines on Hill 881. It was a brilliant war strategy. There was hand-to-hand combat all along the Hill until the North Vietnamese Army consolidated after wiping out the

Marines on the bottom of the Hill. Now, it was double mass force with the North Vietnamese Army halfway up the Hill fighting their way to the top of the Hill for the Marines on the base on top. Maybe, by now, you the Reader see what Vietnam was really like and that was just one battle in The Hill Fights.

The Marines called for massive jet bombs, and helicopter airstrikes on the Hills to try to prevent the North Vietnamese Army from overrunning Hill 881. Pops casually said, we fought for 12 days straight fighting for that hill. I said, "Pops, now you're tripping. Can't nobody fight for 12 days straight." If you could have seen the look my pops gave me when I said that. It was a Vietnam Vet death stare look. He was like, this boy thinks I'm lying. Pops said, "I'm not joking. We fought for 12 days straight! Easy! You fight for a day or two straight until your body just passes out from fatigue from this experience. An explosion or shrapnel hits something, wakes you up and you jump right back in the fight." Pops said that if you woke up and it was nighttime, it was really messed up. You couldn't see and you didn't know who the enemy was and where the enemy was. The only way you knew was when someone shot. He said it looked like Christmas lights and shooting with pops and bangs everywhere. Both armies used tracer rounds. Our bullets were red, and the enemy's bullets were green. Without lights in night battles, this was the only way to know who the enemy was. Pops said after another day or two of fighting, they passed back out from fatigue. Just imagine keeping that cycle going for 12 days. That was how they fought for 12 days straight. I remind you that the Hill bases were there to help protect our 5,000 Marines in Khe Sanh Base. The same 40,000 North Vietnamese Army soldiers also attacked Khe Sanh, the base the hills were supposed to be protecting. It was too hot on Hill 881 to even worry about Khe Sanh at the time.

Pops said one thing he hated about the night fights was listening to the wounded Marines holler, squirm, moan, groan, and call for their momma all night. They couldn't help them because everybody was pinned down because it was too much heavy fighting. If they moved or got up, they could get killed. They saw the horrendous casualties in the morning and the wounded that made it. Pops said the night fights were like watching cartoons. It would be an explosion and you would see a flash. Sometimes you would see Marines in the flash. Sometimes you would see North Vietnamese Army soldiers in the flash.

The base Hill 881 was officially overrun by the North Vietnamese Army soldiers. These same 40,000 North Vietnamese Army soldiers were now going for the kill of Hill 881. They were also on top of the Hill. It was official that Highway 9 was cut off by the North Vietnamese Army. The North Vietnamese Army were shooting down the medevacs for the wounded. To put this in context for you, the Reader. Those 150-man waves of the North Vietnamese Army overran Hill 881. The reason we knew was because some mornings there would be dead North Vietnamese soldiers on top of the Hill. You already see the North Vietnamese Army shooting down the medevacs, so the wounded are piling up with no rescue and time ticking. Pops said lots of Marines died from the shock of just seeing their wounds too long. Pops said those mornings were horrendous. The stench of death was all in the air. They literally saw body parts. They saw dead North Vietnamese looking like China dolls. They could have seen a hand or a leg with no body attached. Even worse, there were so many wounded. A Marine might have gotten his guts blown out, but he was alive with a split open stomach from some explosion. Someone may have placed a poncho over his stomach as the Marine laid down just to hold in his guts. If this Marine stood up, his guts would just fall and hang out. They needed the poncho and compression and medevac, but they were shooting down the medevacs and then there was another night battle. That went on for twelve days straight. When it was morning again, they would see the damages.

Here's the finale of Hill 881. You thought it could not get

worse, huh? Allow me to paint this picture vividly with color. So, on January 19, 1968, the Recon team was ambushed. January 20, 1968, two companies of Marines were demolished on Hill 881. January 21, 1968, the North Vietnamese Army attacked Hill 881 in mass force. They also attacked all the Hill bases and Khe Sanh big base simultaneously with heavy fire. The bases were under attack which meant the Hill bases couldn't help Khe Sanh now. And Khe Sanh couldn't help the Hill bases because they were all under heavy attack. With the medevacs being shot down and Highway 9 being cut off, totally surrounded, there are no troops coming to save them was the new reality. It was not like we had an extra 10,000 or 20,000 infantry units that could come save the front line. Did you forget that there were 40,000 North Vietnamese Army that came across the front line or came from Laos and were all on the South Vietnam part of the front line with the Marines? That would have been just more wounded. So, as you can imagine, the wounded are watching the lifetime clock ticking hoping for medevacs and are piling up in numbers. These same war tactic strategies were used on all the hill bases and Khe Sanh attacks as well.

The Marines on Hill 881 had put all the wounded together on one side of the base. The Marines realized it was either you keep the Hill, or all dies. The Marines kept fighting 12 days straight. On the 11th or 12th day, the Hill was overrun so badly that the Marines had to call an airstrike on their own location. What? Yes. We bombed ourselves to stop the Battle on Hill 881. I guess the North Vietnamese Army felt like they had been fighting for the Hill for 12 days and then the Americans bombed themselves. They may have felt like Americans were crazy. They really wanted Khe Sanh and the Hill's Marines were supposed to be easier to defeat. The catastrophe was when the bombs hit the Hill, you either survived or got killed. The area where all the wounded were was where the bomb landed. Pops said all or most of our wounded soldiers were obliterated; blown to smithereens. No more suffering. This was Vietnam.

That was the end of the Hills 881 battle for Pops. Pops survived, just shrapnel. This was just one battle and it was not the worst battle for Pops. Just keep reading.

To make things worse, the Vietcong and North Vietnamese Army attacked the whole country of South Vietnam all simultaneously on January 31, 1968 which was the Tet Offensive. Do not forget the battle of Khe Sanh on the front line lasted 77 days with those 40,000 North Vietnamese Army soldiers which started January 21, 1968. Bottom line, the Marines were pinned down on the front line. Simultaneously, the Vietcong and North Vietnamese Army attacked all through the country on January 31 for the Tet Offensive. Can you imagine the radio on that day with hundreds of bases under attack at the same time? This was Vietnam.

Back to Hill 881, the North Vietnamese Army retreated after we bombed ourselves or they might have just left and retreated so they could participate in Tet Offensive. Bottom line, they retreated. The Marines got air support and medevacs after the North Vietnamese Army retreated. The U.S. military also started attacking the North Vietnamese Army with mortars and artillery. They were the same ones attacking us at Khe Sanh. I hope no one forgot that Pops was only 18 years old and at this point had only been in Vietnam for maybe four or five months.

I am giving you the stories my pops told me, raw, no cut, no mix. If you, the Reader, have had enough, stop here because my pops' War stories keep escalating until you reach a plateau. I have about five or six more stories like this ahead and it keeps getting worse, but with an unbelievable but true ending. He was caught twice. Keep reading to find out what all happened.

Let's have a timeline check because I don't want to lose you. Pops had just done 12 days in a row in straight battle on Hill 881. Pops joined the fight at Khe Sanh for a 77-day siege. These two were back-to-back which means Pops had just done 80 days of straight battle. Before those 80 days was Bloody Con Thien and before that was the Danang Airport attack. Now let us go forward starting with Khe Sanh Battle.

Exhibit B: Article of Vietnam kids in wagon Khe Sanh Battle

I changed my mind, let us go back. Pops said he clearly remembered when it came over the radio that Lang Vei was under attack. Lang Vei was a special forces unit located a couple of miles from the border of Laos on Highway 9. The Hill bases were maybe five miles from Laos border off Highway 9. Remember the fork in the road ambush. Pops said, then it came across the radio that Lang Vei was completely overrun. We lost Lang Vei. Imagine that psychologically knowing you are next, three miles away and they are coming. Naturally, you know the NVA target was Khe Sanh, but you must pass the Hill bases to get to Khe Sanh. Pops said on Hill 881, you could see Khe Sanh when it was not foggy, and he said he saw Khe Sanh ammo dump exploding. The NVA attacked the ammo dump first just like on the Hills. Pops said he could see the Battle of Khe Sanh like watching a movie on TV for two months every day. Pops being on the Hill, you could just look down in the valley seeing Khe Sanh. Pops said Khe Sanh was taking it hard. They were getting hit pretty non-stop. Pops said he could see the planes and helicopters being shot down the same way they did the Hills. Pops said you could see when it was not foggy, it was monsoon season. Monsoon season was rainy for months. Pops said one thing that was constant was the flashes of explosions hitting Khe Sanh and flashes of Khe Sanh Marines shooting back. There was no helping Khe Sanh by foot. 40,000 NVA on the ground have Khe Sanh base surrounded, the same way they did the Hills. Marines on the Hills could only help by firing mortars and artillery. With Khe Sanh being surrounded, the enemy was moving closer and closer to the center. The closest the enemy got to Khe Sanh was our wires. Yes, they did have a couple of small firefights with Marines on the outskirts guarding the wires. Besides that, none of the Khe Sanh Marines saw their enemy. They saw the enemy's artillery. That was it. Run for cover.

After the first month of the 77 days siege, yes, the NVA had slowly gotten closer all the way up to our perimeter wires. Air support was a problem at Khe Sanh that first month because they kept getting shot down. So, the U.S. devised a plan to keep Khe Sanh supplied. We took maybe 15 planes and helicopters to deliver supplies from just two planes. Some planes guarded other planes; some were decoys. Bottom line, this massive effort for resupply worked. The one or two plane resupply things did not work. They kept getting shot down. As NVA slowly advanced all the way up to our wires after the first month, the U.S. devised another plan that saved Khe Sanh from what was about to happen once the NVA circle closed in on them. The only way that Khe Sanh survived was that we put a ring of steel around the base Khe Sanh. What the heck are you talking about, a ring of steel? Khe Sanh would have been overrun. They have 40,000 enemy troops surrounding 5,000 Marines in a valley. The NVA had crept up so close that after the first month of the siege, they got all the way up to our wires. The only thing left was the call CHARGE. As the 5,000 Marines waited for final charge, daily for the whole 2nd month, around the clock, the U.S. with B-52 bombers, carpet bombed non-stop circles around the Khe Sanh base. The NVA could not get through that circle of bombs around the base. Wow IKR. If it had not been for B-52s and the ring of steel around Khe Sanh, we would have lost Khe Sanh eventually. The U.S. forces could not afford to lose Khe Sanh. It was the largest base or largest concentration of U.S. troops on the front line. The fire bases only had maybe 500 to 1,000 troops. One by one sweep across our front line. Let me paint this picture of the front line of Vietnam as clearly as can be. Vietnam was a long country, as long as the distance from New York to Florida. North and South Vietnam had water on the east border of the Gulf of Tonkin. On the front line of the DMZ, you've got North Vietnam up top with at least 50,000 troops facing South Vietnam. To the west of the front line was the country Laos. North Vietnam has over 40,000 NVA in Laos around the front line. That was 40,000 NVA troops on top north and to the left or west another 40,000 more in Laos. The east was water. America was set up for the front line, one big base mass of troops at Khe Sanh. 5,000 Marines are on the west side bordering Laos. On the east side of the front line, one big base, Dong Ha, with maybe 2,000 Marines and U.S. troops. That was 7K U.S. troops on both corners of the DMZ front line. Littered all through the front line in the middle are 10 small U.S. fire bases. Pops said in Vietnam he went to all our bases along the front line at some point in time. Each of the small base's averaged between 500 to 1,000 troops. But we do have air power.

Okay, enough for Khe Sanh. Hopefully, you see the setup and can do the math. Let us talk about the Tet Offensive. Tet was the Vietnamese Lunar New Year. The Tet Offensive was the largest attack in the whole Vietnam War. The Tet Offensive started on January 31st and lasted two weeks. Pops said between the Battle of Khe Sanh and the Tet Offensive, the War energy changed. The morale changed so much that no longer did U.S. troops think this would be an easy war. As a matter of fact, the energy changed to, could we win this war and why are we here? Even though the NVA lost Tet in the end after two weeks, The NVA won the hearts and souls of their people and also made the U.S. question if the war was winnable. Brilliantly and strategically the Vietcong attacked 100s of U.S. bases in Vietnam on January 31, 1968 between 12:00 a.m. and 3:00 a.m. Two weeks before this, the NVA attacked with overwhelming force at the Battle of Khe Sanh. Pops was not in the Tet Offensive fight because he was at Khe Sanh and the Hill with heavy fighting and pinned down until the 77-day siege was over. Pops and I agreed they were going for the big push. If they had defeated the Marines at Khe Sanh and took over the front line; and, two weeks later the Tet Offensive attacking the whole country, it would have been ugly. Brilliant plan though, you got to give 'em credit. Pops said they were excellent fighters and strategist, more importantly, they were willing to die for their cause, saving or fighting for their country. Pops said they definitely had heart and at times were relentless. Bottom line, after the Tet Offensive, all U.S. soldiers in Vietnam clearly realized we had underestimated the enemy. After the Khe Sanh Battle died down, it was back to normal war with Vietcong and NVA. The difference was that America respected their enemy after the Tet Offensive.

Timeline check. It was approximately March/April 1968 and a lot of soldiers are starting to realize this War might not be winnable. I also remind you Russia and China are supporting and supplying the NVA. Pops continued doing Recon even with this new reality.

Sylvester Bracey, Sr.

Chapter 5

Battle of Dong Ha or Dai Do

Approximately the end of April 1968, was the *Battle of Dong Ha or Dai Do*. Pops said this was his personal worst and most intense battle of the whole War. As kids, this was one of those battles Pops spoke on with emphasis to me and my brother...Dong Ha. I knew for years and decades that Dong Ha was something special. Just for reference and knowing Pops' stories, I went to YouTube the same way I went to YouTube about Hill 881 and Pops saying we bombed ourselves and seeing from other Marines and seeing the video footage. I researched all Pops' stories. I clearly remember Pops saying the *Battle of Dong Ha* was ugly. Pops had also said, no matter how many times you shoot, they just keep popping up.

In 2016, I watched the Battle of Dong Ha or Dai Do for the first time on YouTube. After watching it, I sent the video to Pops via text. I called him maybe a week later and asked him if he watched the video? Pops said, "No, it has been a little busy." At this time, Pops was in and out of the hospital a lot. I simply asked, "Pops where were you in the Battle of Dong Ha?" Pops replied, "we were guarding the bridge until they called us back ASAP." Pops said, "they told us to hurry back, or we might not have a base to hurry back to." I actually saw that part on YouTube. For me to see, that was another story fitting perfectly. Now that I know where Pops was, of course, I watched the video two or three more times. I wanted to follow where the unit assigned to guarding the bridge and all of their actions and what they did in the Battle of Dong Ha. All the battles I have mentioned so far, you can see the fight video footage. The difference was the YouTube vets in these battles are famous now. Lots of them paid well for being heroic, decorated Marine Vietnam Vets. That is why I am writing this book. My Pops never received his true respect for the depths of the Vietnam War he endured. I am telling it all. Welcome to the Battle of Dong Ha also known as Dai Do.

Approximately, 1,000 Marines fought 10,000 NVA and held the line. This battle was a 3-day Battle Royale of Hell on Earth. From approximately April 29, 1968 to May 2, 1968, this battle occurred. The first day of the Battle of Dong Ha or Dai Do, Pops was not involved in the skirmish. Pops was in the Recon platoon attached to a unit on the bridge off a highway. For a perfect reference to when Pops entered the Battle, see YouTube Battle of Dai Do, part 3. I will not comment on the first day of the battle because Pops was not there yet. For you, the Reader, if you want context of day one which was horrific by itself, check out the Battle of Dai Do parts 1 and 2 on YouTube. They are short videos but horrific and give you the setting for what Pops was racing back to help defend. On day 2, Pops' bridge guarding unit was called back to help fight the NVA in masses surrounding Dong Ha. The importance of the Dong Ha U.S. base was they were the supply hub for all the bases on the front line. If the NVA took Dong Ha, they would have effectively cut off the lifeline of supplies for the entire front line. The U.S. could not afford to lose Dong Ha, so we called every unit close by to help with this assault being under attack. The NVA had cut off all river traffic and were in heavy mass all around the Dong Ha base and Village of Dai Do. The enemy was estimated at 10,000 NVA with 1,000 Vietcong guerillas. The Marines were 1,000 and 2,000 South Vietnam soldiers on the way to help. Pops said it was simple life or death. If they didn't make it back to Dong Ha base quick, we might not have had a Dong Ha base, period. Pops knew that if they were talking about overrunning Dong Ha, it had to be huge amounts of enemy troops. Pops said before they left the bridge, the captain gave a life-or-death speech to charge the Marines up. This was the first time Pops was told to Fix Bayonets. Meaning put your bayonet knife on the tip of the rifle barrel, we will have hand-to-hand combat. They double time marched back to Dong Ha. On their way back, Pops said, "We saw the enemy en mass, but command said it's more important to get back to Dong Ha rather than attack the enemy while you see them." At this point, Pops knew if they would not let them fight the enemy they were seeing, Dong Ha must be pretty bad.

Some of our troops did short sporadic fire fights with the enemy as they went around the enemy, but staying the course express to Dong Ha. They made it to Dai Do and linked up with the other marine units. The other Marines had already been fighting one day and told Pops they were all over the place and all the local villages were surrounded. Plenty of casualties and deaths on that first day of fighting an overwhelming force. With all the local villages being surrounded, the indication was that the U.S. Marines base, Dong Ha was the true target. The Marines defended Dong Ha on the first day of the Battle and after consolidating our forces went on the attack to the local villages. The only problem with our counterattack was we did not know the exact size of the force we would be attacking. The Marines didn't learn until after the War the size of the attacking force in Dong Ha.

The mission was to clear out all the local village of NVA troops with all these pieces of units of marines together totaling 1,000 Marines of course air support and artillery from other bases. Pops said the fighting was so fierce as we attacked the first village. The NVA were all around as well as in the villages attacking back. Somehow, we pushed through and secured village 1. Pops said death was everywhere on both sides. Pops mentioned later how we were fighting lots of bunkers in fortified positions. They were enemy bunkers everywhere. We went bunker to bunker killing NVA soldiers. They were about four or five villages the NVA had taken surrounding Dong Ha. The Marines consolidated and went for Village 2. The fighting was so fierce at Village 2, the Marines could not penetrate: so, more marines from another angle joined the attack to penetrate Village 2. Eventually after hours they secured the village number 2. Special note. Remember those 2,000 South Vietnamese troops that were coming to join the fight. The South Vietnamese troops were supposed to cross the river and attack Village 2 from another angle. The Marines tried to wait for the South Vietnamese troops before attacking Village 3. The South Vietnamese Army never showed up. They actually deserted. No 2,000 South Vietnam troops are coming. If the Marines started with 1,000 troops, they are now down to 600 or 700 troops, 300 wounded or KIA.

The main thing I remember from Pops in Dong Ha Battle or Dai Do was Pops said, "No matter how much we shot at the enemy, they kept popping up. No matter how much you shoot." Pops said, "Marrk I could run through two or three rifles shooting so much. The barrels so hot they are turning orange or wouldn't shoot no more, too hot. The NVA still popping up, charging at us and we are dropping 'em like flies. We had to pour water on our weapons to try to cool them off. Instant steam. When we ran out of water, we took turns pissing on our weapons to try to cool them off and grab another one." In this battle Pops said it was hundreds to thousands dead. Pops said "Lots of them died in hand-to-hand combat. Marines versus NVA bunkers. Marrk, they had hundreds of bunkers in Dong Ha Dai Do. We keep shooting at these bunkers until they stop shooting. Then throw a grenade in there, making sure they are dead, next bunker keep moving ahead. This was the scary part." Pops said "you know that game duck hunt on the videos? You just shoot the duck and another one keeps popping up non-stop." Only difference Pops said was that in Vietnam, these ducks were shooting back. Big difference. The NVA kept sending Kamikaze teams running at the Marines shooting and dropping. Pops said the worst fighting was night. You get in your position and don't move unless you are doing a lot of shooting. Remember you can't see nobody. You are shooting at just gun flashes. Green or red flashes all night tracer rounds. Sometimes you hold your fire and only shoot when something was moving or close to you or you hear something close to you. The crazy part you see in a split-second decision, through an explosion or gun flash. Who was moving? As a bomb explodes 20 feet in front of you, but to the left of it flashing there are five NVA soldiers running towards you or other marines and only the flash gave away their position. These were non-stop assaults during the nights in Dong Ha. By the morning time we had secured Village 3. They were other Marines already attacking Village 4 and were almost totally surrounded in a small perimeter calling for backup on the radio. It was actually Pops unit from the bridge who started with 150 Marines. They only had 30 or more left that are not shot or badly wounded. They went to help the trapped marines in Village 4. It was only a few blocks away, so they ran there double time. Guns blazing. They reached the Marines in Village 4 consolidated and tried to continue the battle of consolidating in Village 4 and moving to Village 5, but the NVA were using OVERWHELMING, OVERWHELMING FORCE. Pops said it was just way too many of them and no way for us to be reinforced. Pops said "We were getting low on troops, you know. We had to slowly RETREAT," as Pops laughed when he said that. "But Marrk it was heavy fighting all the way back to that 3rd Village. Matter of fact, they stopped attacking when we finally linked back up with the 3rd Village. They finally retreated back to that 4th Village still in mass. By now, it was another morning, of course there are bodies and body parts everywhere, NVA and Marines. But many more of the dead were NVA, I know that. We didn't find out until after the War, it was 10,000 NVA and Vietcong there. We might have had a thousand troops for this battle but by the time this 3-day battle was over, we might have had 500 troops left, if that many."

In summary, that was the Battle of Dong Ha or Dai Do. The Marines stopped a major assault and attack on Dong Ha base saving the front line from being supply cut off. Just for the record, Readers, Pops still never watched the video I sent him about Dong Ha. I asked him, "did you know y'all were fighting 10 to 11,000 NVA and Vietcong in Dai Do Dong Ha Battle?" Pops said, in his cool way, "I heard something like that, some battalion, but it was never confirmed the actual number. Pops said, but I know in that last village, it sho felt like that cause, I mean Marrk, no matter how much you kept shooting, they kept popping up," as he shook his head. Pops said, "for real at one point, I thought they was superhuman, get shot and get right back up and keep charging. That's how many of them it was. They were like ants." Pops really had not realized how many NVA and Vietcong were there and how outnumbered the Marines really were. Once again, Battle of Dong Ha or Dai Do was Pops' personal worst battle of the Vietnam War.

Timeline check, it was May 1968. The Dong Ha battle was the climax of Pops first tour in Vietnam. Remember Pops was still 18 years old and has been in lots of serious battles at such a young age. This was just from November 1967 to May 1968. Pops cruised through the end of his first tour with no more major battles. I am telling you that Pops' Vietnam War stories kept escalating with Pops being a killer in Vietnam, surviving, and then being released to go home. When Pops got home, he saw a lot of racism in America. The civil rights movement was going on which brings me to Pops' video. He was talking about the racism and discrimination in Vietnam 1970 on YouTube. Pops went viral with over 6 million views. Pops' video was also in The Black G.I. documentary and stored at the Smithsonian Black History Museum. Pops had been in the Black History Museum since he was 19 and never knew it. That was where his video came from. On the video, Pops spoke about some of the racism against Blacks in the Marines and even racism on the bases. On the Black G.I., it was basically a film crew that interviewed Blacks about racism in the Army, Navy, Air Force, and Marines. When they got to the Marine Corp part of the racism in Vietnam to actually see with my own eyes my pops calling out the Marine Corp on the discrimination against Blacks. I was like *Dayummm*. Pops you calling it out over the whole Marine Corp on the Blackness – I was a Proud Son...Period. Pops was clearly the leader in this group. Pops never saw the video. For me, I was already still hurting from his December 7, 2019 departure so to hear his voice fresh; to see him in action speaking that literature video was like Pops being reborn. To see the actual responses on FaceBook and Twitter, the world loved Pops. They were showing him "Mad Love." I said to myself, if they only knew the battles in Vietnam that helped build Pops' views toward racism.

Yes, Pops did mention to me there was racism going on in the Vietnam War on some bases and also racism within the Marines higher ups and the policies. Pops said, yes, some Marines got court martialed and even were sent to Long Binh prison for just giving Dap (The Black Power Handshake). It was just a greeting amongst brothers, like saying hello. Brothers were going to jail sometimes for giving dap or reduction in pay if you didn't stop. On some bases, Pops said, you would see Confederate flags. Pops told the story on his video about going to the USO show where some American singers and actors entertained the troops like Bob Hope, Sammy Davis, Jr, and others. One time twelve white boys pulled out M-16s on a few Blacks Marines. My Pops and the Marine brothers went and got their M-16s and did the same thing to the white marines and was threatened with court martial by higher authorities. Some were told they had to cut their afros. Pops' famous words in the video, "That's Not My Culture." Just making the video, Marines were told they could not wear their jewelry or wrist bracelets. If you watched Pops' video, you would see Marines giving each other ugly dap. Fortunately for them, this was not a Marine Corp video, or they could have been questioned and got a possible Article 15. The video was made by private U.S. citizens. That was why you got a chance to see brothers giving dap in the War. Pops said on some bases, it might be only 30 or 40 Black Marines and it was 300 or 400 white boys. If the Black marines were in a group talking and giving dap, let us just say it was 15 of them together, someone would tell the authorities and here come the Military Police (MP) or the riot squad saying break up this crowd or you could get in trouble. Like a write-up or Article 15 where they take some of your pay. Pops was like "for what? We are just brothers talking to each other. When white boys were in groups, they never said that. Only to the brothers." At some point, Pops started noticing we were being treated unfairly, the same way we imposed our American racism on the Vietnamese people. Pops started realizing the Vietnamese people just wanted to come together and unite as a country and not a divided country, North Vietnam and South Vietnam. Pops said America was the one that put a puppet over South Vietnam in the first place. Those people just wanted to come together as one nation. Yes, there were factors of racism in the War and they went all the way through to Marine policies. Pops said, "yes, we had fraggin' over there." What's Fraggin'? Fraggin' was, say you got a white racist on the base, but it's time to go to the field and just so happens we get ambushed or enter an enemy attack. Some of those racist white boys did not make it back. I am not saying no names. You know what I mean. Friendly fire incidents did happen. I will leave it at that. Another Fraggin' would be the officers that sometimes were new or do not know this War yet were giving suicidal missions in the field. You told five Marines to go check this out while seasoned veterans of the war knew and saw the set up for a Vietcong ambush attack. Somehow once the battle started that officer somehow got killed... That was Fraggin'.

Pops said they could do that racism shit on the bases, but in the field, it was no time or place for racism and any marine would prefer to have another marine with him no matter what color just to provide the NVA more targets besides you being the only target. Pops said plenty of times it might be a Black man that takes the heat off your ass while you are under attack. It might be a brother saving you out there, ambushed or treating your wounds making sure you get medevac to the hospital. Pops said, "A lot of white boys learned the hard way.

Lots of them changed their views realizing you just saved their life and vice versa. Lots of the white boys ended up being best friends with brothers after incidents like this, but not all of them. That was my take on racism in the military. This does not include racism back home or our racism towards the Vietnamese people. Marrk, they killed so many innocent people that was not Vietcong, you would not believe it. Burning down their houses or hooches, just because that was the order given by the authorities. Look at it this way. We were in **their** country, killing **them**. I am going to sit that right there for a minute."

At this point in the War, Pops was considered a short timer. Meaning, you got a month or less to go in a one-year tour. Short timers do not want heavy action because you are eligible to go home in a few weeks. Remember Pops was drafted into Vietnam, no choice. Short timers wanted a smooth last month. Feeling like they served their time, they wanted easy going, stay out the way, cruise through that last month of their time in Vietnam.

Hey Reader, this was your *Intermission*, Pops has completed his first tour in Nam and headed back home. It was approximately early summer 1968.

Pops at home, Southside Chicago, Illinois

INTERMISSION

Pops was back home. I cannot talk about what I do not know. I do not know exactly how long Pops was at home or all the events that happened while Pops was at home. I do know from hearing from Pops when he came home, the civil rights movement was in full swing. Racism was heavy in America for all to see. There were fights, protests, and marches. I figured Pops must have gotten into some small trouble or skirmishes on the racism front here in America. America did not know where Pops just came from and what he had been through. His words verbatim were "When I came home, they were protesting the War and racism everywhere in your face. It was so much racism bullshit going on, I might as well go back to Vietnam where I can shoot people legally." Whatever Pops saw that summer of 1968 at home, made Pops go back to Vietnam with an attitude to let off some steam. Pops was back in Vietnam 1968-1969. Just for the record, Pops has a younger brother, joining the Marine Corps. My uncle only went to Vietnam to go fight with his brother. I have heard over the years, they tried to reach each other in the War, but never hooked up in Nam. My uncle was down by Saigon, the Capitol. My Pops, Sylvester Bracey, was all DMZ, the front line. Special note, somewhere around this time Martin Luther King was shot and assassinated. Lyndon Johnson, the President who was a heavy backer of the War, had resigned on national television. Meaning the main person pushing the War, just quit. I just held your hand through Pops' first tour in Vietnam. Remember Pops has not been caught by the enemy yet!

MARKUS BRACEY

THE SECOND TOUR

Chapter 6

Ashau Valley The Walking Dead 1968-1969

So, Sylvester Bracey, Sr., Marine Recon was back in Vietnam to vent a little and did not like the racism he saw at home. When Pops came back to Nam, he was about 19 years old and considered a Veteran of the War to the other Marines and U.S. forces due to his battles in his first tour. Pops got mad respect for being an Old Timer at 19 years old. Pops got his props going into his second tour. Pops still did Recon his second tour. This was where my timeline gets a little fuzzy. Approximately May 1969, one of the missions Pops was given was the Ashau Valley. Hey Reader, did you see the movie, The Walking Dead or Hamburger Hill. That was Ashau Valley. This was a battle where the NVA came in from Laos, another country, did their attacking in South Vietnam and retreated to Laos. Stick and move, stick and move. Going into Laos was a violation of the Geneva Convention. The battle for us was to try to catch the NVA in mass before they retreated into Laos.

Another point I need to emphasize was that the 82nd Airborne Army went into Ashau Valley en mass, 10 battalions of infantry, but they also had the 9th Marines. Although the 1st Battalion, 9th Marines do get credit for assisting in The Walking Dead, my pops was 2nd Battalion, 9th Marines that did the recon. Listen closely, fact; no marine infantry units had Recon. But all our attacks en mass were reconned first, meaning, Pops was attached to the 1st Battalion 9th Marines or 82nd Airborne just for Recon or reconnaissance. Keeping it simple, Reader, doing recon means that Pops had to go in first. Whether the recon team saw the enemy, were ambushed or went straight through, my point is that Pops was there in Ashau Valley, Hamburger Hill, and the Walking Dead doing recon. Remember sometimes they let the recon team go through just to get to our troops en mass. Pops was there and he doesn't get the credit! My Pops told me he was there. We watched The Walking Dead movie and Pops said, "That was us." He gave details on the side all through the movie. Pops did not get his credit for being there in that battle. To put a cherry on top, Pops told me a couple of times they had to go back to save those Army boys. We had already gone through, came back, and sent them in. We let them know the dogs got the scent heavy. Go clean it up. They were getting hit pretty bad, we had to come to save their ass or their ass was out. So, I ask you, Reader, who did the Recon for 1st Battalion, 9th Marines, and 82nd Airborne in the Walking Dead? That was Pops, 2nd Battalion, 9th Marines attached to the battle for Recon the same way with Hamburger Hill. Pops said verbatim, "I was there, doing Recon." Okay, maybe you don't get it. Let us talk Ebonics. From Pops' perspective... "I go in with a 7-man Recon team. We do our job. Locate the enemy. We fall back to a safe place and let you go in to do yo' job, clean it up, clean 'em out. They get to beating yo' ass bad. We can hear it on the radio. So, we got to come back in, throw a surprise ambush attack on the enemy from another angle to take the pressure off yo' ass. Army getting hit hard. Naw, they can't say, I wasn't in that battle. I went in the first hour before them, and I had to come back to save their asses. Yeah, once again," in my pops' cool voice, "I was there. They might not have made it if we didn't come back, and that's a fact." I am smiling wishing you, the Readers, could have heard Pops talking to me about this. But when we saw the movie, Pops gave me the details and confirmations. So, add to Pops' credits *Ashau Valley*, *The Walking Dead 1969* and *Hamburger Hill*. We watched Hamburger Hill too. Pops said a lot of it was phony but also a lot of it was real and gave details as the movie went on.

Timeline check. Pops has been back in Vietnam a month or two, 2nd tour. Pops said one time when I was doing Recon in the jungle over by Laos border, they caught me and my team. I said, what you mean they caught you? Pops said, "what you mean, I just said they caught me. I think that's pretty self-explanatory." We laughed and he passed the joint as we were speaking. Time out now, I am going to give you a little of the personal Pops. Yeah, we smoked weed regularly all through life. Matter of fact, Pops was the first person to smoke with me and my brother when I was 16 years old. I thought that was the coolest thing on earth to be able to smoke weed with your father and your momma didn't know anything about it. It was just cool stuff; it was just weed.

This next part was all just Bracey men stuff. Thinking about it reminds me just how much I miss my pops. So here we go. When I was 21, my mom gave me and my brother a house to live in. We just had to pay her rent. My Pops had gotten in a little trouble with the law and was in Cook County jail fighting a case and had been there like six months. Pops said he was going to trial because he was not copping out. When we found out Pops was there, they were offering house arrest but he had nowhere to go. Instantly, my brother and I got Pops setup for house arrest to live with us in Jeffrey Manor on the southside of Chicago. This was the first time we lived with Pops since we were babies 1 and 2 years old. It was cool stuff, we kicked it heavy. My brother was working, I was working, and Pops was at the crib. Even my older sister, Nikita, came from out of town when Pops lived with us as well as my younger sister, Asia. We had sessions every day. It was common to talk about Black issues and the War. My Pops talked casually about making bombs or even a zip gun. In his cool voice, he would say, "You just need an ignition, a charge, and a source and sometimes a timer." He gave simple details regularly. Some products you could just get from your local hardware or grocery store like ammonia mixed with something. I forgot what he said to mix it with but he would be like that's a bomb. It will definitely explode.

Let me go back a little. We had been having sessions, our brother talks all of our lives. It would be my brother and I and sometimes even my cousin, Derrick, listening to Pops and we all chimed in on Black issues and freeing ourselves. This was all before 21 years old. We would have my mom drop us off at these different apartments and we would kick it, brother style. Lots of time, my pops, my brother and even, Derrick, would go over to my Uncle Crib's house. We knew session was in order when Uncle came around too. Oh My God, if you could see how my pops and his Vietnam brother, my uncle, greeted each other with DAP you would be amazed. All you could see and hear was blap, blap, blap, blap, blap, blap, blap, blap, fist bumping and knuckles cracking. Just watching them do the handshake with some seriousness was the coolest thing in the world to watch. Until this day, all our lives, my brother and I, my uncle and even Derrick give Dap every time we see each other. A lot of times in these sessions, we would play games while smoking like Stratego and even Risk war games. Over 70% of the time my uncle would win the game. Uncle told me when I got about 40 years old. "You know why I win most of the time in Stratego?" I said, "Why?" Uncle casually with a smile said, "I cheat!" I said, "Aww, wow." Uncle said, "Hell Yeah! I would move my flag if you were about to win or close to it. The object was to win the game. Don't forget that." I said "You dirty. That was dirty. You would be cheating us all this time?" Uncle just smiled and said, "I won, didn't I?"

Special Note. I also remember when Pops was around my uncle. Those are times they might speak about the tortures in Vietnam. They would tell stories of them cutting off your fingers, knuckle by knuckle, trying to get captured Marines to talk. They would tie you up naked, light your pubic hair on fire and let you burn for a while. They even placed men in cages in water ways in Vietnam that were filled with hungry rats. The G.I.'s head would be out of the water watching the rats swimming all around while their body was submerged and tied up being eaten alive by rats. Even slicing you up with razor cuts all over you and putting salt all over you to make it sting. Electric charges to fingers, even genitals, your private parts. I mean this was real Vietnam torture they heard while there or through recovering the dead bodies. These are the stories we heard. As kids we knew Vietnam was no punk. You either survived and fought or you did not survive.

Back to the weed. I forgot Pops smoked plenty of weed in the War. He was in the jungle where it grew freely. It was 100° every day and plenty of rain for half the year. Pops said their stuff was great. Even on the Black market, G.I.'s bought marijuana. Pops said you would get a bundle of 20 huge joints the size of your fingers, but super long for $5.00. That might be a half ounce in today's weed for $5.00. I told you, I am giving you the raw and uncut. At one point, Pops was flirting with the hallucinogens. He said, "Yeah, I was tripping in the War." I think he said LSD, I'm not sure, but yes, he was definitely tripping. I really think he was on a trip in the Battle of Dong Ha when he said he would shoot 'em and they got back up, superhuman. Enough of that.

Pops told us these stories in the same cool swagger you see on his video. He had the exact same smoothness. My brother and I used to play games acting like Pops about any situation. Just reciting how Pops would have said this. Yes, I can sound just like my pops and tell you stories how he would say it. But, my brother, Sylvester Bracey, Jr., he was identical to Pops' swagger. He has the same voice, same coolness, same swag. I would get an A for acting like Pops. My brother would get an A or an A+ for acting like Pops. His voice was naturally Pops. I am a great actor who listens to details, but for my brother, it was just natural. So, my brother moved out in love when he turned 21 years old. Then it was me and Pops and he was off house arrest. My brother still came by pretty regularly just for sessions. In late 1990's, I moved to St. Louis. I invited Pops there just to get away from Chicago. Pops came to St. Louis where we lived together and worked together at jobs for maybe three years. Then I came back to Chicago while Pops stayed in St. Louis for most of the rest of his life other than the three years he came back to Chicago and lived with me in Chicago Heights. My uncle also lived with me and rented a floor in

Chicago Heights. By this time, my brother had been married 10-15 years doing his thing doing married life with kids.

My point was, I had maybe 7 to 10 more years of living with Pops than my brother. Obviously, I got way more stories and details of the War. Don't get it twisted, over a lifetime my brother got plenty of the War stories in detail, I just got 7 years more. I am probably the only person, besides his widow wife, Bridgett who slept with Pops, so she heard the nightmare stories, waking him up in his sleep. I truly do not think anybody can give you intricate details of Sylvester Bracey, Sr. War stories with a timeline better than me. So, I am sharing them with you now raw and uncut.

Back to the War. We left off at Pops telling me, "I got caught like I said, that should be pretty self-explanatory," and we both laughed as he passed the joint. I said, "What happened?" Pops said in his cool voice, you see on the video. "Well, Marrk, I was running Point. Yeah me, Point man. I am leading my Recon team in the jungle and I came up on an embankment. You know, where you got to step up maybe a few feet in this mud. And uh, as I came up, I'm trying to get my balance, you know on the even ground Recon team right behind me. Then they popped with an ambush. We had about 15 Vietcong with all 15 rifles up and pointing at our heads. We walked into an ambush. When they popped up, they said in good English, 'Drop your weapons!' They had the draw on us. We trying to just make it up to the embankment, a few muddy feet, a few seconds, they got weapons up and pointed. One second. They had the draw on us. Stunned, we froze for a second. The Vietcong said again with a little more anger, 'DROP your weapons! This was all happening within a 10 to 20 feet perimeter. We are close with 15 rifles aimed at our heads. Now, of course, the thought runs through your mind of trying to pull some Rambo movie shit. But this was the real deal. Trying to beat their trigger pull with The Vietcong rifles already up. Naw, I'll pass on that one. I know the third time they said, 'DROP YOUR WEAPONS?' We dropped 'em." Pops said,

"Once we dropped the weapons, a couple of Vietcong picked them up while we at rifle gun point, hands up. They corralled us in a group and started talking crazy about the War. Like, 'why are you here?' The Vietcong asked. They were using war propaganda asking, why were we fighting the white man's war."

On this Recon team, Pops had a couple of South Vietnamese soldiers and a few white guys. As we go into this next part, Reader, remember the Vietcong said, "Brotherman, *This Was Not Your War, Go Home.*" They were speaking directly to Sylvester, my pops. Pops said, "I heard 'em, but I didn't want to make a move, soon as I move, they might shoot me in my back. They shouted again, 'Brotherman, *This Was Not Your War, Go Home.*' I got the point, this time I had heard rumors from other Marines sometimes they let the brothers go. So, I started walking away with no weapon. The Vietcong shouted 'RUN!' So, I started running. I could hear them physically assaulting my Recon team. I did look back for a second and saw somebody got hit with a rifle butt. I kept running. This all happened within a 2-minute timespan. Then I heard the shots as the AK's sprayed my Recon team. All of them killed...KIA.(Killed In Action)" Please Reader, remember this turning point in the War and just imagine if this was you. Pops made it back to the base unharmed and reported the demise of his Recon team. Pops said we sent out Marines to recover the bodies that's how I knew they were killed. Okay, the Marines pat you on the back, and say good job for making it and surviving. They give you a couple of weeks off duty, time to clear your head, you know. But, in this off-time, Pops had re-evaluated his whole situation.

Timeline check. Pops was only four months into his second tour. He got roughly seven more months to do in Vietnam. Let me help you understand this clearer. Pops, was off duty, recovering mentally from the Vietcong ambush. The Marines were about to say you're healed, time for the next Recon mission, but the Vietcong said, Brotherman, this isn't your war, go home. Pops was conflicted about the War at this point. The

Marines were ready to send me back for more Recon. The Vietcong say, don't come back out here. Pops knew the reality was that if he went back out and was caught again, he would most likely be dead. Pops also said, you got to have respect for a man that spared your life at gun point. Pops was a Libra; it was all about balance and being fair. Pops was definitely conflicted. Pops was also noticing the Vietnamese people just want to come together. No north and south, just one Vietnam. Pops was also questioning himself with all this War he has been through. Why are we here? The Vietnamese people never did anything to him personally? They are the ones that just let him go free after catching him in the jungle. I can only imagine the fear of going back out when it was not resting well with Pops' spirit; it was unsettling. We are truly at a fork in the road for Pops Marine Vietnam War and life. What would you do? You can't go AWOL. You are in the middle of a war in their country. You don't want to go back out doing Recon. The enemy, Vietcong spared your life. America just wants you to go out, they don't care if you die. You don't want to go to prison or jail, you could have stayed in America for that, fighting in the civil rights movement. Did you forget, Reader, Pops was only 19 years old making this huge grown man decision about what was next for his life. What would you do in his shoes? Let me remind you, I said Pops got caught twice in the jungle. This was only the first time. I told you Reader; Pops' stories keep escalating from worse to worser to the worst. We are almost there, keep reading.

CHAPTER 7

JOINING THE SOG

So, it was approximately 4 to 5 months into the Second Tour in Vietnam and Pops was 19 years old and about to make one of the biggest decisions in his life. After being caught by the enemy in the jungle and his Recon team was assassinated, Pops was given a few weeks of R&R (rest and relaxation). Pops really did not want to do Recon in Vietnam anymore especially after the Vietcong spared his life and let him go free. The Marine Corp was ready for Pops to go back into action and Pops officially let them know he does not want to, at least not Recon in Vietnam. Anything else, Pops was open to doing, besides Recon in Vietnam. Pops had enough. So, the Marine Corp pulls Pops to the side and said, the higher authorities are offering you a job in a Special Operation that requires no more Recon in Vietnam. But there was one catch to it. Pops asked what was the catch? If you agree to take this special operation, 1) you have to sign a contract and 2) you have to promise you will never talk about this operation for 20 years or you risk being persecuted fully by Military Court Justice System. Pops was a little puzzled. They said, you will be put in a Studies and Observers Group (SOG). Pops said all I got to do was observe and never talk about it. They said yes. Pops said as long as it's no more Recon in Vietnam, where do I sign? Pops agreed and signed the contract. Pops officially signed the contract to be in the Studies and Observation Group (aka SOG) or SOG team Special Forces.

Timeline check. It was five months into his second tour. Pops was now a member of the Studies and Observation Group, better known as the SOG team. Pops figured for the next seven months, he was just going to cruise through Vietnam and observe things. With signing this contract, Pops could not tell anyone, not even other Marines or Recon buddies. You can't tell anyone, anything, about this for 20 years. Pops was 19 years old, and now just waiting for orders on what he has to observe in the War. Let me give you some background Reader so you understand what just happened. Google or YouTube Vietnam SOG Team. Pops was a little naïve and still at 70 years old, did not know exactly what he had just signed and gotten himself into. For you the Reader, I will just be blunt. Pops just joined the most dangerous and elite force in the Vietnam War. The unit Pops just joined, the SOG, are even above Special Forces and Navy Seals. My Pops went all the way to the Top, Top, Top and still never knew at 70 years old. In 2016 or 2017, I told him after I studied the Studies and Observation Group. So, I called Pops maybe 2016 this was before I researched and knew the details of SOG teams. Here was my call with Pops in 2016. I will try to be verbatim. "What's going on Pops? Nothing much Marrk just in and out of these hospitals. I actually got a stint in me now, but I'm cool. Nothing I can't handle". Pops was going through some heart procedures at this time. Pops said, "you still coming down to St. Louis to make the video right"? I said, "yeah, I'm still coming, I haven't made a solid date though." Pops said, "Okay, cool". I said, "Pops what happened after you got caught in the jungle"? For you the Reader, we had recently been talking about the War. We have been doing this for years, really all of my life. Pops was like, "just come down and get it all at one time on video that way you got it all in one shot." Just letting you the Reader know, I was just doing a follow up on maybe a conversation we had weeks before. So, Pops was answering what happened after he got caught.

Pops said, "well you know Marrk, after getting caught like that and they let me go. I really wasn't feeling that Recon in Vietnam no more, not that I was scared, but more out of respect for a man who had a AK47 to my head and told me to go home and spared my life. You got to respect a man like that, you know. And even more, the Vietcong ain't really did nothing to me personally except spared my life while they killed my Recon team. I'm cool with the Vietcong. Looks like to me they just trying to bring their country together. We the ones bombing, killing, and burning their houses down. For what? Vietnam ain't never did nothing to America but fight back and they are supposed to. It's called self-defense." I said, "so what happened, you still had 6 to 7 months to go? Well, Marrk, they came to me with this Special Observer thang once I told 'em I wasn't doing no more Recon in Vietnam and I meant that." Pops said, "I told them I'm not disobeying orders, I just don't want to do that no more and I got my reasons, find me something else to do." Pops said, "They picked me to be in this Special Observer thang, but they said, I had to sign a contract and never talk about it for 20 years. Pops said, "As long as I didn't have to do no more recon in Vietnam, I was cool with it."

Pops said, "one thing that was strange was they had us going into Laos and I knew weren't supposed to be in Laos. Laos was neutral country, you know." I said, "We were in Laos"? Pops said, "Yeah they had us doing Recon down the Ho Chi Minh trail in Laos. Yeah, I was wondering myself, why they had us in Laos? But when I was there one time, we saw Chinese troops, marching down the trail." I said, "Chinese troops? What's China got to do with this?" Pops said, "That's what I'm saying." I said, "Pops are you sure these were Chinese troops? Pops emphatically said, "Marrk, these were Chinese troops." I said, "How do you know?" Pops replied, "Because they were tall like us. The NVA and Vietcong are little people, maybe 5 feet to 5'8" feet. These troops were more like 5'6" feet to 6'3" feet, and they were fresh. They looked good I must say. Another thing they wasn't dirty. These were fresh tall troops with fresh new uniforms, marching in mass columns. Yeah, Marrk, these were Chinese troops. I said" what were they doing there? Pops said, "I don't know, and I wasn't about to find out. Pops said, "My job was to be a Special Observer and that's what I'm doing, observing." I said, "wow, that's interesting" as Pops said, "Look Marrk, the nurse is here. I have to get off this phone. Let me know when you coming down, so we can take care of that business." I replied with my usual, "Got you Pops. Love. One, I'm out."

Reader, Reader, Reader, if you YouTube studies Special Observers Group Vietnam and SOG teams pop up. In my research, I find out the SOG team was a covert elite operation of special forces teams. You could not volunteer or join SOG team, you had to be picked to be a SOG. All members of SOG team Vietnam were either special forces, Green Berets-Army, Navy Seals-Navy, and a few of the best Marine recons. This was a covert elite Special Ops group consisting of a combination of all the best in different regular Special Forces. Bottom line this as the Top Commandos of all branches of the U.S. Armed Forces that are in Vietnam. So, as I am reading about these SOGs, it said at some point in 1968-1969, the SOG had a 100% casualty rate. It also said 100% either POW, AWOL, wounded casualties, or death. The SOG team wore no American insignia on missions. They didn't even use American weapons. So, for you Reader, no U.S. Marines on your shirt, no sign of you being a Marine. Just basic camouflage in another country. Hey Reader, if you can't tell by now, yes, I am triggered about this SOG operation. I am full speed ahead studying SOG. Of course, I couldn't wait to call Pops back after I studied so we could compare notes of what I have learned as well as what he did as a SOG team member. You might have noticed, I called it Special Observers. The real name was Studies and Observation Group. I also found out even to this day, the U.S. government has never acknowledged we had SOG teams. This would be a violation of the Geneva Convention.

Back in Laos, if SOGs were caught, they legally could be personally found guilty of committing War Crimes. By the way even my brother Sylvester Bracey, Jr., will naturally confirm we heard this story as kids. My bro will confirm Pops saying he did

Recon on Ho Chi Minh trail and seeing those Chinese troops. He will also confirm Pops saying the NVA was coming down the Ho Chi Minh trail like it was the Dan Ryan Expressway in Chicago. My bro is going to find out the real depths of what Pops was doing in Laos in this book. I compared notes with Pops when I called him back weeks later to hear some of his missions in Laos. This SOG operation was so covert and secret that there were only 7,500 SOG members in the whole 10-year Vietnam War. We only had 550,000 troops total in the Vietnam War. SOG team members didn't even talk to other SOG team members about their different operations in Cambodia and Laos. The only way that SOG team members would whisper amongst other SOGS with different missions was the casualties, the deaths, the KIA's, the Killed in Action. Let me say this part again. Being a SOG in 1968-1969, the casualty rate was 100% death, wounded or AWOL. That was a hell of a number. The more I studied the more my gut told me Pops really didn't know what he was into, but he was doing it following orders.

Pops had struck out already being caught by the Vietcong and not wanting to do Recon in Vietnam anymore. This was his last positive option. The more I studied SOG, the more my gut was feeling like they kind of tricked Pops into taking this death mission. Yeah, I know he signed the contract with limited details, but I truly think Pops thought he was getting something easier than Recon in Vietnam trying to save his own life. He really was not trying to do something much more dangerous. Plus, with him being a Black Power leader in the Marines, authorities may have been like, send his Malcolm X ass across the fence. In Vietnam to Vets, Laos and Cambodia was called Crossing the Fence. I might sound a little repetitive, but I want you to understand the depths of where we are. Being across the fence, you might as well say, you are doing Recon in North Vietnam. Yeah, it's that serious.

First of all, the NVA was not supposed to be there. After Dien Bien Phu where the NVA whooped France's ass out of Vietnam in the 1950's, that was basically the reason we were in the war. In satisfying all parties, North Vietnam was now accepted as a sovereign nation and agreed to split the country in two parts, North Vietnam and now South Vietnam. Before that, France ran all of Vietnam and treated them like slaves in their own country for decades. Because France lost, America stepped in. At the Geneva Convention, after it was agreed in ink, all of you fighters of Vietnam can go to North Vietnam, everyone who wants democracy can go to South Vietnam. Ho Chi Minh, the actual leader of the NVA just wanted all of Vietnam to come together with rights for the People. Winning the war and kicking the French's ass, he inherited half of the country legally. Ho Chi Minh was North Vietnamese. He had a formula as their leader. He was willing to give up ten men to every one man from any enemy attacking Vietnam. Let us do the math. In 1970, there were 40 million Vietnamese people. America sent 500,000 to 600,000 troops to Vietnam. In using Ho Chi Minh's formula, Uncle Ho knew he had to lose 6 million people at 10 to 1 ratio to get America out. Uncle Ho knew eventually America had to fold unless they were willing to kill all the 40 million Vietnamese people. America tried to pull the same thing, they did with North Korea and South Korea. Divide them and install a puppet government that would assist and label the other side as bad or communist. You see the resemblances? It worked with the Koreas. They just pulled it again with the Muslims with 9/11. We were cool with Saudi labeling Iraq bad, then we took Iraq. They were trying to do it in Iran and Afghanistan the same way today. See the similarities?

Now back to Vietnam. Ho Chi Minh was not going for it as you see. They were totally united and no countries big or small have attempted to attack Vietnam since. With the Geneva Convention giving Ho half of the country, Ho Chi Minh had a base to consolidate and operate. *Special Note.* My Pops' hero of all time was 5 feet, 110 lbs., Ho Chi Minh. Now that you see Ho's formula you should clearly understand why there was no way we would win the Vietnam War. Killing all 40 million

Vietnamese would have been genocide. Now let's go back to the Geneva Convention and Laos. Yes, Ho Chi Minh signed the war truce and accepted half of the country, but his goal was to unite all of his country and people with rights. They had been slaves to France for decades since early 1900s, so this wasn't over for Ho. Here comes America sticking our neck in it. These people just wanted freedom and rights and were willing to die for this cause thanks to Ho Chi Minh. So now America helped establish so-called democracy in South Vietnam. The North was Ho Chi Minh. Cambodia and Laos were both on the west sides of Vietnam. The east side was water. The DMZ (De-Militarized Zone) was a 5-to-10-mile neutral zone between North and South Vietnam. All countries agreed to keep the conflict down and not enter Laos or Cambodia.

The North did not honor this part of the Agreement and America sent the CIA to Laos to train Laotian soldiers just in case. America never sent mass troops into Laos and eventually noticed, once we were in the War, a lot of the NVA attacks came from Laos or Cambodia. Because we had no mass troops in Laos or Cambodia, no boots on the grounds were the reason the SOG team was established. America needed to see why these mass NVA troops were attacking from Cambodia and Laos then retreating back to Cambodia and Laos which was off limits per the Geneva Convention to American troops.

Hopefully, you see by now this was way over 19-year-old Pops' head. Pops was just trying to be a good Marine. Pops had risen all the way to the top. He had fought battle after battle and was just trying to stay alive and go back home. Pops actually was concerned with saving his own race, the Black People of America. Pops felt like maybe he could teach our people characteristics and tactics to free ourselves from America's racism, but that was another story. So basically, Ho Chi Minh cheated with the Geneva Convention. He signed it but never honored it while America was pouring troops into Vietnam ready for War. We were so-called protecting South

Vietnam from North Vietnam and the spread of communism. Yeah, okay, keep believing that American people at home. The reality was Ho Chi Minh was just uniting his people by any means necessary and he did it. That was it. I am setting you up for Pops' mission as a SOG in Laos. I am giving you the Vietnam War from my pops' perspective raw and uncut. The big picture I got from Pops after the War. All those years I guess I learned a lot from the bro smoke sessions we had. I am about to wrap this part up and get back to Pops' missions as SOG in Laos and the rest of his 6 to 7 months in Vietnam. Okay, let us do some geography.

The front line of the DMZ neutral zone on the North Vietnam side, the NVA have at least 100,000 troops. On the east side of Vietnam, you got all water. On the west side of South Vietnam, you got Laos on the upper part with at least 50,000 NVA troops and on the bottom part of South Vietnam west you got Cambodia with at least 50,000 NVA troops, and all through South Vietnam was littered with Vietcong Guerillas that we don't know who's enemy and who was regular civilians. Now you got the real set up of the Vietnam War. The only way for America to know what's going on in jungle-filled Laos and Cambodia was to violate the Geneva Convention sending in these special forces recon SOG teams to see what was going on. By the time I get through with you Reader, you will understand the Vietnam War with a new reality. I remind you we only had total 7,500 SOGS during the whole 10-year war and China and Russia are supporting North Vietnam with supplies and ammo during the whole War. The most SOGS we ever had together at one time was 2,000 SOG. Let us do some math, put 1,000 in Laos and 1,000 in Cambodia. What the hell can they do with 50,000 NVA in Laos and 50,000 NVA in Cambodia? EXACTLY, Nothing Walking Dead in time.

By the end of the Vietnam War, out of 7,500 total SOGS, only approximately 1,800 lived and survived.

Back to Pops. After a little studying and researching SOG, I called Pops back. I'm ready. Hey Pops, what you know about Macv-SOG? Pops laughed and said, what you know about Macv-SOG. That was us when we went into Laos. I will say you are a good student Marrk, what you got for me? I said, "Pops, did you know when you joined SOG team, you joined Special Forces? Pops said, "I don't know, bout no special forces. We were Special Observers. But we were on a special operation in Laos. Pops said, I told you they made us sign for this operation. You can never talk for 20 years". I said, "Pops tell me some of the things you did in Laos". Pops said, "I already told you we did Recon on the Ho Chi Minh Trail. I know I told you bout the Chinese troops and they were maybe 30 feet away marching down the trail in mass formations. We were on the side of the trail they didn't know we was there". Pops, what was something else you did or saw in Laos? Pops said, I saw so many NVA troops that I knew America don't know what they got coming. Marrk, the NVA was coming down the Ho Chi Minh Trail like the Dan Ryan Expressway in Chicago. Every day, different times, heavier traffic. Yeah, I could smell their cigarettes in the wind. I can hear and see 'em talking to each other. Pops said, Marrk, you got to remember Laos was a neutral country, the NVA doing things and acting freely. Pops said we were 20 miles inside the border of Laos ain't no U.S. troops around, ain't no U.S. bases around. They comfortable being themselves. They don't know we are here maybe 20 to 30 yards away and we cammied out. I look like a tree, straight camouflage. And of course, I don't want them to know we are here. Marrk, you got to understand. I'm looking at tank after tank after tank, platoons of tanks. Artillery after artillery, after artillery pieces. Troops in formation and more troops in formations and literally watching battalions going down the trail towards Cambodia and we out there for some days until it's time to pull back and head to designated LZ (Landing Zone) for pick up. I didn't want no trouble, its 6 or 7 of us, sometimes hundreds or thousands of them and we are 20 miles away from South Vietnam on foot, that was a lot of jungle to be running in, if you get spotted. I'm like, wow, Pops. This sounds crazy as hell. Pops said, "I know, right. Yeah, they told us things we could do. Sometimes, they told us things to do, like a grab and snatch, bring back a prisoner or calling in airstrikes. Pops said, me personally, I was just trying to observe, make it to the LZ and come back and tell them what I saw. Pops said, I had already heard about calling in those airstrikes. When you call in those airstrikes, they know you are there. Somebody had to give them grid coordinates. They also warned us when we joined SOG that if the enemy spotted you and you were surrounded or being chased by mass units. Call in the Airstrikes. It took me a minute to catch on, but you basically would be calling in airstrikes on your own position. So, for me, I was just trying to observe and stay alive, leave that Rambo shit to them white boys. I said, Pops, you are crazy. Pops laughed and said, aww, you just finding that out. At this point, I knew my pops was a superhero.

Timeline check. Pops had approximately 6 months left in his second tour and he had been doing Recon as a SOG on the Ho Chi Minh Trail for about a month across the fence. America had come to the realization through the SOGs that if we didn't do something about this Ho Chi Minh Trail, the War would be 50% harder to win. At the same time, we attacked the Ho Chi Minh Trail more and didn't even think about amending the Geneva Convention to put U.S. troops out there. That's expanding the War to three countries instead of one. Hopefully, Reader, you are starting to see the picture of how unwinnable this War was. Pops has the birds-eye view doing the Recon. I told you, Reader, Pops stories keep escalating and we are still not through. Six months to go. Aw hell naw... ah hell yes. Got to survive for six more months. This was Pops' Vietnam raw and uncut.

By now, if you are reading this, you know Pops was lucky to be alive. He had lived through a hundred deaths, maybe a thousand deaths. All this at 19 years old. Remember when you were 19, Reader, LOL? Yeah, we remember, Writer. Just get back to the story, you are dragging this out. What happened to your Pops? Okay, Okay, we are at six months left. Pops said, "They wanted to add a new member to my team. It was something about this guy. This white guy. My instincts didn't naturally connect. I mean, I had no problem with the man. I don't even know him, but something was, you know, not right. I welcomed him in and let 'em know I'm the point man. I asked him if he had any problems with that cause I didn't want no mishaps out there in the jungle." Check this out, my pops a decorated Recon Marine was telling a Green Beret or Navy Seal in SOG, he was Point Man. "I can't remember his name," Pops said, "but he looked and felt like the gung-ho type. I let him know we are just going out, we going to be out there a few days so prepare well. We gonna just observe and come on back." Pops told him, "Ah yeah, they gonna be out there." Has anyone noticed Pops was calling the shots for his SOG Team? He was a True Leader. Pops said, "the white boy looked at me, like how I know they gonna be out there?" Pops said, "If you scared to go, don't go because I need somebody that's got my back." Pops said that charged him up a little bit.

To you, the Reader, Pops got a vibe like dude was scared, but he didn't want a Black guy to show him out or outdo him. So, Pops was running point man and I didn't tell you. Pops ran Point Man all through both tours. He said he enjoyed running point. Even my younger bro will verify when we were kids, Pops, saying, "Ah yeah," in his cool way. "You know, I had to run Point" (then he gave you the look with a smile). Pops took pride in running point plus Pops told us he didn't like to depend on what the next person saw, that's unless we got attacked from the rear he jokingly said. Bottomline, he had a feeling about this new white guy on his team. Sooo, they went out. This was Pops' last Recon mission as a SOG on the Ho Chi Minh Trail. Wait, let us go back. As a SOG, the authorities were suggesting that Pops calls in airstrikes when he saw these mass enemy troops. Pops said he was downplaying the numbers sometimes when he reported what he saw just because they want you to call in airstrikes on the enemy. Pops' view was like "I am the one 20 miles across the border, Not YOU!" Pops said, he was like, "Hell Naw. I ain't calling in no airstrikes unless I have to." Pops wanted as little contact as possible. He also said, "My job was to observe. You had plenty of situations like that in the War where somebody sitting back on a base nice and safe **telling you what you should do or be doing while you out there in the field with the enemy**. He said, "I know how to make life and death decisions for myself. I don't need nobody back on the base telling me how to get killed," as he laughed. The base authorities wanted NVA in mass because that's less NVA we got to kill later and yeah, I understood that. I am laughing now cause Pops said, **"But It Ain't You Out There With Those Mass Troops, It's Me."** So yeah, airstrikes would be for Pops, only if needed for self-defense.

So, they were on a mission to observe the Ho Chi Minh Trail in an area where planes saw a lot of movement. Pops said they got about a football field away from the trail. This was not like when he saw the Chinese troops 20 feet away up the ditch on the trail. Pops was at a distance. Pops said, that they looked like ants out there. He said it looked like they were doing construction on the trail. It was more than usual. Pops said you could see troops coming through, at different times, even artillery pieces like platoons carrying artillery pieces. Pops said, "Now remember, we are just a football field away. We can see them, but they can't see us in the jungle watching them. They had snipers in the jungle too. We had seen a few on other missions, but they didn't see us. Of course, we let them walk and keep on walking. I am trying to have as little contact as possible. We are across the fence. Ain't no U.S. bases, ain't no U.S. mass troops, ain't nowhere to run to and if you make contact, you got kill 'em and kill 'em quick. You don't need that noise out in the jungle. Plus, all those troops on the trail. I could only assume that NVA Recon snipers was out there for us. It's no other U.S. troops around." Pops said, "We watched them all day. We moved a couple of times, but still stayed about the same distance. They were doing a lot of digging, like they had villagers come out and work on the trail, but they were still going through there, them troops. They might have been repairing some airstrikes or even making a detour. They were doing a lot of digging like ants. Pops said after watching them all day, white boy signals to him, he wants to call in airstrikes. Pops said, "I signaled back pointing to my eyes, pointing to them and I cross my neck you know on that airstrike." Pops said, "The white boy signaled back to me that he just called in an airstrike. I had to confirm what I thought he just signaled. So he went over to the white boy about 20 feet away." Pops said, "I thought he was asking me was it the time to call for airstrikes. The white boy was telling me he just did." Pops signaled for extraction and called for the helicopter. Pops said we had 15 minutes to make it to the LZ landing zone. He said, "But I know them airstrikes gonna be here in 5 minutes." Pops left and said about 5 minutes later, he heard the jets. Couple more minutes, he could hear the airstrikes in the background. Pops said he stopped and looked for about 5 seconds and it look like somebody just blew up an ant farm. They all started coming our way towards the jungle. It looked like hundreds. Pops also said he wasn't used to running around in the jungle fast like they were doing then. He said, he liked smooth operations, not rush jobs. Pops also said, "I guess white boy thought we were just gonna sit there and watch the show -- The Hunt for Us. "

"Yeah, we made it to the LZ. We made a small perimeter, about 5 minutes later you could hear the chopper coming. As the chopper got closer, we also heard gun shots, not at us, but like someone close was trying to shoot at the chopper." Pops said it was probably them NVA recon snipers. "Chopper landed, we got on," Pops said. The pilot told Pops and crew someone just tried to shoot at them. They saw some flashes. They took off in the chopper headed back across the fence to South Vietnam.

This experience affected Pops. He said, "I'm better off by myself." I think this was Pops' last SOG mission. I don't remember or he didn't tell me how he went AWOL at least the details of it. Pops just said, "I went AWOL for 6 months in the jungle." Because that sounded so crazy to me, I didn't ask specifically how he walked away. All I know was Pops said as simple as day, "I went AWOL for the next 6 months until my tour was up." I said, "You lived in the jungle for 6 months?" Pops said, "Yeah, I lived in the jungle for 6 months. It ain't that hard. You can do it too. I had already done a month in the jungle before doing Recons where they just drop off yo' supplies so yeah, I lived in the jungle of Vietnam for 6 months." I said, "Pops, how you gonna live in the jungle? In a War?" Pops said, "I felt like I had a better chance of survival by myself. Just to make it back and I did." So, Pops was in the jungle by himself in a country at war and full of war during these times. Pops said his real motivation was to get back home and fight for Black people's civil rights in America. At some point during the War, Pops figured it out. The Vietnamese were only fighting to be able to vote. They were fighting and dying for their civil rights. Pops believed in that because besides being a Marine and being an American. We got the same fight.

CHAPTER 8

THE SEARCH FOR PEACE

Pops had officially drawn the line at 19 years old that he was no longer fighting to keep these people oppressed. Pops was on his own in the Jungle of Vietnam with 6 months left in his 2nd tour. Hey Reader, this was still, Vietnam. So as Pops wandered through some of the most uninhabited parts of the jungle in Vietnam just trying to survive, Pops ran into a Vietnamese woman in the deserted jungle. When Pops saw the woman alone of course he was scared, and she was too. Then again, Pops was heavily armed, 10 grenades, 10 full metal jackets. Pops only knows a few words in Vietnamese, and she knows no English. If you saw my pops' video, you will know how cool Pops was. Pops somehow charmed the Vietnamese woman. They communicated like cave man and woman. Pops was definitely worried like where was the rest of them, her family, her friends, the kids. Through sign language, cave man style, she told him America bombed her village and killed her family. She just had one brother left. To make a long story short through caveman styles, Pops lived with her and began having a relationship. Yes, it was very possible that I have a half-brother or sister that was Vietnamese. Pops told me and my bro her name, but I can't remember it. All I do remember was Pops earned her trust over some weeks and months and she likewise earned his trust. At this point, Pops was eating animals cooked over a fire as well as different plant soups. Sometimes they had rice. Pops was basically eating what she ate. She had been out there for a while already. She had one small hooch on top of ground and one small tunnel room underground. Pops said the room was super small about 8 feet by 8 feet and only like 5ft tall. Pops said it was small but enough to survive in.

Hey Reader, let us be realistic for all the War that Pops had been through, he finally had some relief. Pops said it was peaceful living with her. Every now and then, they would hear our bombs hitting the ground in the distance. This was an area in the woods that not even NVA troops or U.S. troops were there but it was still in Vietnam by the frontline just the uninhabited part of the jungle. Pops had recuperated over a couple of months and felt as if he could make it or at least survive this way until his time was up. Pops was totally off the grid and probably considered MIA (Missing In Action) or KIA (killed in action). The Marines or SOGs hadn't seen Pops for two months. I am assuming, Reader, that Pops got low on supplies or was tired of eating whatever they were eating. One thing I forgot Pops did was find the weed (marijuana) growing in patches, so he had plenty of weed. Unlimited amounts. But Pops went out to find the closest base to go resupply. Pops did, one man Recon headed back to the closest base, remember Pops has Recon maps, so he knew general directions. The problem was just not running into any Vietcong soldiers or NVA. Pops was so lucky; he did find some U.S. troops after walking some hours "that way." Seeing U.S. troops hours away from his hidden location, Pops popped up saying don't shoot, U.S. Marines. They asked him to identify himself as Pops hollered, "U.S. 3rd Division, 2nd Battalion, 9th Marine Recon team. They killed my Recon team." The soldiers embraced Pops and he joined them on patrol and went back with this group of soldiers to their base camp. I don't remember what unit found him or what base camp they took him to.

You've got to remember that his last mission was with the secret SOG team, so no one had any information on Pops. Pops met with someone, one of the officers that asked how long you been out there? And go clean yourself up, get you something to eat, we'll meet later at such and such hours. He told Pops that he was going to try to find Pops' unit. You, the Reader knows that Pops didn't want to be found and Pops last unit was the secret SOG team. Of course, Pops did not mention he was a Special Observer. Pops loaded up on supplies. Pops hooked up with some of the brothers to find out where some brothers that was on perimeter security detail. Before the officer could come back and find where Pops was supposed to go or be, Pops was gone again. Pops went on and met with the on perimeter detail and let him know at almost gunpoint if he had a problem with it. I'm otta here, as they let Pops venture back into the jungle by himself. Reader, I already know, you don't have to tell me, this sound crazy as hell. But this was my pops' story.

After two hours of self-recon, Pops made it back to his new home in the jungle with his Vietnamese girl. Pops said she was so happy when he came back. By this time, she was speaking a little American and Pops was speaking a little Vietnamese. They were communicating well by then just using the primitive means and sometimes sign language. She was loving Pops as he was unloading. He got soap, food, meals ready to eat (MRE), even chocolate candy for her. All kinds of supplies that he could use in the jungle or at least as much as he could carry. Pops has three more months to do in this Jungle hiding out. I told you Reader, Pops stories are amazing and just kept escalating. I wasn't ready for this smooth landing.

Pops was at peace with himself, loaded and ready to just do three more months in this jungle and Go Home and fight the real battle...Blacks' civil rights. Pops actually wanted to do just like the Vietnamese people and fight for our rights at home. Maybe a week or two after Pops got back in the jungle, something mysterious happened. Pops said one afternoon he was sleep laying up in the underground hooch room and he said he felt like I was dreaming and heard something. Two or three minutes later, he did hear something for real. It's a group of Vietcong soldiers coming in the tunnel entering the room. Hey Reader, you didn't forget I told you Pops got caught TWICE by the Vietcong, did you? Umpf, as the chaos took over. Does this roller coaster ever end? Let me tease you Reader. I know you weren't ready for this one – me either. You can imagine me hearing these stories from Pops like this was the craziest thing I have ever head in my entire life. Pops' Vietnam War stories were always, Oh My God! Pops talking to me in the spirit right now. Saying, wrap 'em up Marrk, wrap 'em up with a ribbon on top. My Man, by the way, make it Black, Red and Green. And I am telling Pops in spirit, I got chu Pops. Pops saying, My Man, Good Man, My brother P, Pops called bro Sly Baby, me and Pwee at that time because we were maybe 8 and 9 years old or younger the first time we heard the last story, the woman, AWOL 6 months story. Yeah, my brother was there with me listening to this as kids. Even my cousin, Derrick all under 10 years old heard this story twice. Pops getting caught by the Vietcong. You can naturally imagine the teen years. More stories in depth.

We didn't know what we were really hearing as far as history, but We Loved It. Pops was a Black Warrior on the battlefield. Straight Black Super Pops hero and cool ass. I literally can't find a word to describe how cool my pops has been all his life in every form, and you can imagine. My Pops loved the creator and Black unity. That's it. Tell "em Marrk, Pops just spoke in spirit. Pops wants to speak to you the Reader.

"Marrk, let me speak to 'em for a minute. Let me holla at the people since this was My Story. You know, well Marrk, you did a pretty good job. I must say. Some of the things you are talking about Marrk, the people need to know. So many of our People are programmed to believe the first thing they hear, then when a brutha' come with the truth, they don't want to believe it. That's the fight, you know. Vietnam wasn't No Punk, and I didn't even tell Marrk everything. You can't, it's uncivilized, but Marrk does know enough to make an impression on the People. You see, it's like this, I know what I went through over there. I learned from it, it actually changed my life, you know.

One thing, I learned over there was that oppression was everywhere. The system trying to oppress the people. But the main thing I have learned was America could be beat, and an Oppressed people if they unite and fight back can beat the Oppressor. We never lost a battle over there, but we didn't win the War. My only wish was that my People learn something from this and use it to your advantage. Everybody got to deprogram themselves sometime. This was a universal thang not a man-made thang. I told y'all, I was coming back in the video. " I said, "You through Pops?" I asked in the spirit. "Yeah, I am through," Pops replied.

I am going to take you all way back. I was the son born into conflict. Yes, Pops was in the hospital room when I was born 1970 fresh out the War. You got to imagine the tension, Pops fresh out of Vietnam, talking lil crazy, Black Power to the max, mom was pregnant and didn't want to hear nothing about the War after all he had been through. I was in the incubator born into conflict. I have an older sister, Nikita, one year older. I have a brother Sylvester Bracey, Jr., one year younger. I have one more younger sister, Asia. So, maybe this isn't a coincidence that I am the one writing. I am a child of the Vietnam War. Let's go further, my brother and I use to march in circles and sing the marine anthem, Halls of Montezuma and hut 2, 3, 4, hut 2, 3, 4, hut 2, 3, 4. I asked my mom in maybe the year 2000, 20 years ago, I said how old were we marching for Sylvester. Mom said, that was when we were living together, so you had to be under 3 years old. Probably 2 and 1 years old. Reader the thing was, I remember that vividly, I was 2 years old.

When we were 2 to 5 years old, before kindergarten, a few times, white guys in Black suits came over to my grandparents' house looking for Sylvester. Reader, we were 3 and 4 years old, we didn't know the CIA was looking for our father. All we knew from mom was some type of authorities were looking for Pops for something he did in the War. As babies we still took Pops' side in wondering why they were looking for him. If you can't tell Pops was already our hero in our baby years. We just couldn't understand it and needed clarity. We didn't know

Pops had some unfinished war issues. He was only around the first two years; after that, he was gone. He would pop up maybe once a year, but when he popped up, it was magic. Pops' here.

Reader, I just want to give you some background. The CIA used to come to my grandparents' house and I clearly remember it. They used to come looking like the insurance man that come out to houses except these guys always had on Black suits, white shirts and sunglasses. Hey Reader, why was the CIA looking for my pops? My family and I always naturally assumed it had something to do with the War and most likely something about Black Power activities. That was what we thought for decades. But it was through my research on Pops' War stories that I figured it out. Remember Pops went AWOL on SOG. The only people in Laos from America back then were plain clothes CIA and SOG teams. Couple of factors here. America was not supposed to be in Laos. Pops signed that contract, was he back home talking? Pops went AWOL. Pops after going missing, the records showed him on a base shopping or spending money then he disappeared for a few more months. He popped back up when it was time to go home and was back in America loose. Yes, the CIA wanted to talk to my pops or even try to get him charged for going AWOL. Plus, the Black Power factor played a role in it as well. Was he going to start a revolution? All these factors are accurate. Since we are here, does anyone want to go back and know what happened when he got caught the second time? Remember the Vietcong had just woke him up, walking into the tunneled room while Pops and his female Vietnamese friend were sleeping. It was mid-day, about 2:00 p.m.

Timeline check. Pops had 2 ½ months left in his second tour of Vietnam. He had been AWOL for three months already after being caught the first time and joining SOG team. Pops thought he had it made; just live in the Jungle of Vietnam for six months and be done. Well, the Vietcong had another plan. Pops said, as they walked in, the first thing he was thinking was, she SET him up. Five Vietcongs walked into an underground hooch. How did they know we were there? Let me just give it to you verbatim from Pops as I or we heard it. Raw and uncut – verbatim, I remember it well.

"Well, Marrk, it was a normally peaceful day in the jungle. We had eaten our little breakfast and did our little morning activities. Beautiful day, I must say. I had smoked my greens. Average day, you know, I'm chillin'. We decided to go take a nap, lay it down for a while. Seem like right after I got into a deep sleep, I thought I heard something like I was dreaming. Next thing I knew, I did hear and see something. The Vietcong are coming through the little tunnel and walking into this small room that we have been living in, you know. Instantly, when I woke, chh chh, I locked and loaded. My back against the wall. She started screaming, they didn't move. I said you better tell 'em something or I'm spraying all y'all. Remember Reader this was an 8 ft. x 8 ft. room, very small, 5 ft ceiling. Pops said she screamed and screamed. Pleading with the Vietcong, she even spoke in English sometimes, so Pops could know. She screamed, "Defector, Defector, No War, No War," in English to the five Vietcong in his room with him and her. Yeah, it's kind of crowded in here, easy to spray." Pops said, "She was picking up stuff showing them what he brought like pop, soap, food as she kept trying to convince the Vietcong that Pops was helping her and wanted No War."

Don't forget Pops was locked and loaded on automatic against the wall with the big eyes. The scared eyes. The, I will kill you right now Eyes! You better listen to her! Pops said she was talking and screaming so much, but it was like she knew them, which could have been a good or bad thing. I didn't know yet. Reader, do you remember when the Vietcong caught Pops the first time. They had the draw on him first and they let him go. This time Pops has the draw on five Vietcong with 5 AK 47s right there in front of him. Pops said after a couple of minutes of pure chaos, they looked like they were getting it and started looking at Pops after every item she picked up. Like in sign language saying, he brought me this pop. He brought me this soap, he brought me this food and they looked at the American food and looked back at Pops. The Vietcong clearly seeing Pops was scared for his life and listening to her, plus Pops was one trigger pull away from killing all six of them. They nodded their heads okay and started retreating out the tunnel one by one. The last Vietcong stayed and talked for 5 to 10 minutes to her. They embraced and hugged as they talked in Vietnamese. Pops still locked and loaded just pressure down a little bit because she had gotten to the Vietcong. Pops after watching with intrigue like she was talking to him, like she knows him. Pops said, "who was he?" Pops pointed sign language at the dude saying, who was that to her? As she said in English, "That's my brother, Lam." Pops said, "That's yo brother?" As she happily smiled and said, "Yes, that's my brother."

    Close call Reader. It doesn't get no closer than this one marine trapped in a hole with five Vietcong all armed and all walked away, unshot and unharmed. You got to remember the other Vietcongs let Pops go and killed his whole Recon team that wasn't Black. Pops just returned the favor and gained more respect for them and from them. In the room, my pops was being formally introduced to Vietcong enemy soldiers. Lam, this was Brother Bracey, Brutha' Bracey this was my brother, Lam. Sorry Reader, I might even have a half brother or sister over there, but I can't remember her name. But I clearly remember her brother Lam's name. Once again, Reader, I know this sounds too amazing. My brother, Sylvester, Jr., was a witness and was sitting right next to me hearing this as kids under 10 years old. We heard it several times. I don't believe no other Vietnam Vet can tell you that story. None!

    To wrap this story up, yes, the Vietcong acted cool with Pops, even after they all were out of the tunnel, out of the room. Pops was still on alert, but the pressure went down some after they realized all Americans, just don't want to bomb, shoot and kill Vietnamese people and that was why they were fighting us. So, Pops gave them a pass and they gave Pops a pass as they returned into the jungle. Now, it was just Pops and her again. They are gone and you got to imagine, it was kind of uneasy. Did she do this? What if they come back? Pops said, "She did a hell of an acting job to convince them, BUT? Big but??? What now?" Pops couldn't fight his mad feelings at this point and packed up to move out. She cried and begged and begged him to stay trying to get his trust and security back. Pops couldn't take the thought of them coming back at any time during the next 2½ months downtime to go back home.

Timeline check. It was 2½ months left in second tour. Pops just got caught for second time by the Vietcong. Luckily, it was her brother. As Pops packed to leave his jungle home, he was upset with her for not telling him that she had a brother. Pops said she said planes bombs boom, boom her family. She didn't say that she and her brother were the only survivors and her brother joined the Vietcong, and I came to the jungle to hide and live. Through all this, Pops could not shake his attitude and she cried as he left for good. Pops was back in the jungle by himself trying to let 2½ months tick by so he could go home and begin his fight for our People. Pops had officially learned from the Vietnamese people a way that works when dealing with racism and system oppression. Pops just had to make it 2½ months. Just survive. You probably could have guessed it with all the feelings in the air, Pops didn't go far from her, maybe a football field or two. He could still see his old home as he did Recon around her area at a distance for the next week or so. After a week or so and playing the tape over in his head, Pops went back. He popped up on her a week later. Well, well, well, you are still here, as she smiled and ran into his arms. Pops said, "VC Vietcong come back. Yo brother Lam, did he come back?" She said, "No. No VC, No VC come back. No." Pops asked again, same thing, as Pops settled in an unloaded. Pops was back at his jungle home; Pops had two months to go home. After all this drama of the last two weeks, they both re-accepted each and no the Vietcong did not come back his last two months in Vietnam. All peaceful. They only saw the planes, heard the bombs in the distance while living in a small world inside of the War world they were in. Pops next departure from her after two months was his final departure from her and the Vietnam War.

Let's close this on out Reader. I told you in the beginning it was going to keep escalating. I wasn't lying as you see. I told you in the beginning, you have never heard Vietnam War stories like my pops. The Brutha's perspective. I wasn't lying there either. You be the Judge. I told you in the beginning, Pops was a hero to have survived all of this. As you can see Pops could have died thousands of times in this Vietnam War. Some of you will have views about Pops' service and lack of service in Vietnam and that was fine for debate. One thing, I remind any Reader reading this. Pops was 18 and 19 years old making all these decisions. What would you have done at 18 and 19 given all these life-or-death situations? What would you have done? Would you have followed more orders, maybe even did more Recon in Vietnam? And end up possibly Dead? Would you have done your other six months with the SOG team? And end up possibly Dead. Would you just turn yourself in for military justice and say I'm not fighting anymore? I mean keep it real. What would you have done if you were in Pops' shoes? Pops had already seen enough death for 100 lifetimes. Pops said, "We couldn't dream of the amount of death he saw in the Vietnam War." I say, "Pops, I am glad you are a thinker and started to deprogram yourself to save your own life or else I wouldn't have the pleasure of writing this story." To most, my pops' Vietnam War experiences from the brutha's perspective sounds like a movie.

Pops' stories are exceptional and a magnificent test of survival. I tried to keep it as simple as possible, no big words, no perfect story. Tried to keep it simple from a narrator's perspective. I personally thank Pops for his service for our country and for giving me this gift to share with you, the Reader. If not for Pops telling me and me telling you, you would never know. Most people don't know half of the things that went on in Vietnam. Pops said, "THIS IS ONLY HALF!!! For me, the Vietnam War was too uncivilized to tell the other half. Put it this way Jack, look here, imagine what I just said and take 30 seconds. Stop reading. I said Vietnam was TOO UNCIVILIZED for me being in Recon to tell the other half. Recon goes EVERYWHERE and ANYWHERE!" Recon is normally behind enemy lines and Recon sees ALL FIRST. Yes, this book is things I've experienced in the Vietnam War. But this is truly the watered-down version of the things I've seen doing recon through my own eyes. This is a great learning experience to grow from.

Pops told me in the spirit to leave you with this. *In my story find at least one thing that you can learn from. Just one thing and make that change in your life and I'm happy. Sometimes they might not be happy with your decision, but it's about making a decision that was best for you and your life. If you can do that for me, I've done my job here on earth. I'm out.* So, to close his departure off, Reader, let us finish this in peace.

Last timeline check. It was days with under a week left in Vietnam, second tour. Pops happily and sadly had his last mad love session with his friend, his Vietnamese girl, the woman that helped him, nourished him, loved him, and protected him the last six months of the War in the jungle. Sad moment, but gotta go. It's time. Pops left as the tears poured. She knew and he knew that this was the last time they would probably see each other, and it was. Pops headed back to find the closest U.S. base. Pops popped up on the base saying my time up send me to Danang for shipping home. Of course, the base authorities looked up his name and only found MIA for six months under Pops' name. So, Pops was like, "What you mean, MIA? That's what they got me listed as, as you see, I'm right here. Go back to my entry date as Pops told him his entry date. The entry dates matched as they sent Pops to Danang Marine Headquarters and said let them figure it out. Pops got to Danang same thing. You listed as MIA. Pops said the same thing. I don't know how, I'm right here right now and entry level dates match. So, the authorities said we are not going to hold you back trying to figure all this out. Thank you for your service, Marine, Go Home. Hope I see you again when I get back. Wouldn't want to keep anyone in this Hell Hole." Pops was on a flight on his way back to America for good.

Sylvester Bracey, Sr.

Chapter 9

Final Summary

Hello, Readers. I am Markus, first son of Sylvester Bracey, Sr. I wrote this adventure you just experienced. I hope you have a new appreciation of the perspectives of men serving in the Vietnam War. I'm sure there are a lot of questions, opinions, thoughts, and feelings. Before we enter the cage of opinions, I need you to challenge yourself and ask yourself, what would you have done if you were 18 and 19 years old and in the exact same position Pops was in? What would your decisions to survive have been? I just gave you a synopsis of two tours of the Vietnam War shared with me from my pops. Of course, everyone feels differently, and everyone uses different means and ways to make sure they survive. My point was before you challenge some of Pops' decisions, know the cards Pops were dealt and the hand he was playing simply trying to survive. I remind you when it comes to survival of your life, it's your call not anyone else's. It's your decision and consequences in your life not anyone else's. So, Pops made his decisions and what he thought was best for his survival in the Vietnam War. Guess what? It worked for Pops. He survived the war and lived until December 7, 2019. Let's be fair in our assessment. If Pops had listened to others and the chain of command, there was a great chance Pops would not have survived the Vietnam War. Let me give it to you raw just the way Pops gave it to me.

"Marrk, I had to go AWOL (Absent Without Leave). They left me no choice. Marrk, you got to understand this. If I wanted to go to jail, I could have stayed in the states. If I wanted to go to jail in the military, that option was there as well as an easy option with all the racism. So, jail was not my option; but it was an option. Marrk, I Just Wanted to Be a Good Marine – That's all. I've done everything the Marine Corp asked me to do. All kinds of life-threatening ordeals. I've lived 100 deaths and lives just in the Marine Corp in Vietnam. Once I finally learned the truth in Vietnam, that the Vietnamese people were only fighting for their right to vote, equal rights, a united Vietnam, not south and north Vietnam. Just Vietnam. Of course, my energy changed. I wanted to be Good Marine, but at the same time, I didn't want to oppress these Vietnamese people of their Natural Rights. Pops said, we got the same fight against systems of oppression. Plus, They Let Me Go. I ain't got no problem with the Vietcong or NVA. America does!"

Pops also mentioned that when he joined the CIA's SOG Team, it was different. "The Recon was the same except you couldn't call for troops. No Reinforcements Coming. This was Not What I Signed Up For. Marines come to get Marines even if it's just the body. Marines are coming for other Marines. On my SOG team, I'm the only Marine we got 3 montanyard tribal troops and one other U.S. special forces team member. Another thing with the CIA group SOG team Special Observers Group, they told me after I signed up call in Airstrikes on myself if I'm ever surrounded by the enemy in mass. They would prefer to kill the enemy and me, and say, I was never in Laos. Just being in Laos during the Vietnam War was considered War Crimes against the Geneva Convention. We, the U.S., weren't supposed to be in Laos and the U.S. telling me we are not going to back you in Laos if you get caught. As if I just came from America by myself to just fight the Vietnamese People. ***This Was Not What I Signed Up For***. Marines come get Marines even if it's just the body."

Pops finally realized that he was no longer with his Marine buddies on this SOG Recon Team. Because America was not being straight up and on some other stuff, Pops decided for his survival this war was not best for him and went AWOL. The last straw for Pops was when the other U.S. Special Forces called in Airstrikes in Laos on the Ho Chi Mingh Trail on the North Vietnamese Army (NVA). Pops said when the bombs hit, the NVA dispersed, and all entered the jungle looking for the SOG team that called the Airstrike. Remember there are no troops or U.S. bases in Laos. So, who gave the grid coordinates for this Airstrike 30 miles into Laos? The NVA knew the SOG team was somewhere close by. Pops said, "This was when the Hunter became the Hunted. Ain't no fun when the rabbit got the gun," Pops words verbatim. Pops said, "Remember the movie Platoon at the end when the NVA caught Lyus, as the helicopter flew away?" Pops said "It was just like that except we didn't leave no man on the ground. All troops were present and accounted for in the helicopter. The amazing part was from the helicopter as you are being shot at, you can see just how many NVA troops were hunting for you and your Recon SOG team." Pops said, "it was hundreds of NVA in Laos maybe thousands and it was just our 5-man Recon SOG Team. What if they shot the helicopter down while coming to pick us up? It wouldn't have one Lyus, but 5 Lyus's and a pilot stuck in the jungle with no pickup coming and no chopper overhead to see what happened to the left behind troops. Just an untold story of deaths in the Vietnam War. Not me. Not this Brutha. I made a decision at 19 years old to go AWOL and save my own life, and that's what I did. I made it back home. Not everybody who listened to them made it back home. Remember you can't blame them for your life, that's why it's called **Your Life**. So have your opinions. I know what I experienced and what I did. Some things I am proud of, some things not so proud of. By the way, if I didn't mention it, these stories, I've told my son and sons are only half of what I experienced in Vietnam, but enough to let the people know. I told Marrk, I couldn't tell him everything that happened in Vietnam. Why? Because some parts of the Vietnam War were uncivilized. You got to remember, I'm the one running point man doing Recon all over the jungle on the front line. The things I've seen no one will ever know. Imagine hearing a voice in the jungle saying, help me and as you get closer, you see a tied-up U.S. soldier, split wide open, but alive. I could see all his organs. Other soldiers lay there dead while they were tortured. A solider was saying shoot me, kill me, as the rats, flies, and maggots devoured the body of a living U.S. soldier. What do I do when it's this bad?? What can I do?

At another location while doing Recon, I found soldiers tied to a tree, tortured, and beat up. All their fingers, joints and knuckles cut off. Just palms, no more fingers and knuckles. Even from our side, it was uncivilized. U.S. troops, cutting off ears was a big thing over here. You could see soldiers with 5 or 6 ears on a string, like jewelry. Do you know how gory it was to cut off a dead man's ear? This kinda thang, this Vietnam. Yeah, Vietnam was uncivilized, but I've told Marrk enough to let the People know how it really was in the Nam. Another thing to All Vietnam War Veterans, y'all know what it was like over there. It depends on where you were at, as most of us saw heavy action, some of us saw very little or no action in Vietnam. As you see, I got action all through both tours. We all view the War through different lenses and different experiences. I can't tell your story, the same way you can't tell mine. The only people that can tell my stories are my Recon teams, me, and my sons. Remember you weren't there next to me when the event happened. I'm just sharing my experiences of the Vietnam War through my sons.

The challenge was this, Reader. Can I make a decision to put myself first, to save my own life at 18 years old to go all-in for freedom? I did and I went AWOL. What major roadblocks or hurdles in your life that may cause you to go AWOL on something to put yourself first? Make sure you survive. Realize it's not about them and what they say or want and it's only about you, what's best for your survival. Everyone has an AWOL moment in their own life. Do you follow them or your first mind? I followed my first mind. I made it back. Everybody that listened to them, didn't make it back. On that note. I hope you learned and enjoyed my stories."

Peace and Love

Bruthas and Sistas

Just for the record if you didn't know a Black War Hero

Now You Do.

My name is Sylvester Bracey, Sr., Marine Recon, 3rd Division, 9th Marine, 1967-1969 Vietnam War. You can believe what they told you, or you can listen to a person that was out there doing Recon. They can never see what we saw.

Sylvester Bracey, Sr.

Sylvester Wore a Coat of Many Colors

Yes, Sylvester was a dreamer.
I compare his dreams to Joseph wore a coat of many colors.
Sylvester dreamed the unusual. That's one color in his coat. His thoughts transcended the ordinary. He was a prolific writer, he was intelligent and expressed himself well. From being a reporter on the 8th grade chit chatter newspaper 2 Days Later writings on numerous subjects, he could pin thought to paper (he was exceptional as a writer.
He created his own language.
Who takes the time and patience to do this, he did! (He was a detailed thinker)
He was an architect.
He planned a walled Community long before Trump's wall was even thought of. And he did so in intricate detail which from an aerial view, the complex was shaped like the continent of Africa.
He was a visionary.
Sylvester dreamed the impossible - That's another color in his coat.
He dreamed and plan to survive a nuclear attack on America.
This was at 14 years of age. He played an underground bomb shelter. He listed the number of gallons of water and non-perishables, foods with the longest shelf life, canned goods and dry goods, dehydrated foods, etc. He planned the generators, the batteries, blankets, clothing, first aid kits, tools and building supplies. He even determined how long we would have to stay underground before attempting to go up side. At 13, I believe he was my best chance of survival in this event and determined to be somewhere near him if it happened. (He was brilliant)
He created his own Lottery system breaker. It is all about the odds and that's just what Matt and that's just math he would

say. Did I mention that he won science awards every year in school. (He was so smart - having both mathematical and scientific mind)

Sylvester was an artist - that's another color in his coat. He would create art out of the simplest things a twig or a shell or a rock. From that piece of wood, he would envision an ornate carving and then he took his time to produce it. Sylvester could paint. His love was to create things of beauty. He always acknowledged quotation marks things of beauty. (He was so creative.)

Sylvester was a teacher - that's another color in his coat

He was a huge proponent of self-study. He refused to learn based on the public school curriculum in high school he did a self-study on black history and actually could have taught it. He would say, "Knowledge is it's own reward." It was from him that I learned about Papa Doc, Francois Duvalier, who was the president of Haiti for many decades I learned that he assumed the presidency of Haiti at age 19 he was the world's youngest president. Papa. Also gained Sylvester's respect because he was a black nationalist. He sought to promote and maintain a black race identity four black ancestry and pushed empowerment of black communities. (Sylvester was self-motivated)

Another color in his coat; if you knew him, you would know that Sylvester was a huge advocate for black power. He believed that black should have their own, own their own businesses, support their own communities. Separate was fine with him. He believed that Revolution might be the only answer to equal rights for blacks. (He was culturally motivated.)

At 22 after much study, his dream was that our family of four relocate to Easter Island, one of the most remote inhabited islands in the world. It is located in the Pacific Ocean. It is known for its hundreds of huge monumental statues Built by people of Polynesian descent. It was considered a place of high spiritual power. Potentially, a place where he might have gained political prominence. (He always felt he should rule somewhere). However, he planned to start by forming there. He believed we would grow sweet potatoes and chickens. (I vetoed that plan). But that didn't stop the dreamer, he always had another idea, new dreams.

I think of him as he voiced his many ideas, his many Visions like the beginning of the national anthem he would say "Oh say can you see" our response may have been "I'm right behind you" but we were not. He was so far ahead, we cannot often be at the same pace with him, or see to the extremes that his eyes could see. His vision was so high above us that we cannot really visualize what he saw so vividly. It was too fabulous for our comprehension. Sylvester's coat with a rare garment. I will now say a kingly garment. He dreamed a myriad of dreams all in color. The coat he wore was his multiple anointing; his anointing to use his talents. His biggest desire was just park and others, to ignite their own creations and to use their talents to create a legacy to be passed on and for all you who knew him, hopefully, he was a success!

Remembrances from Angella

Pops (Sylvester Bracey, Sr.) and Mom (Angella Allen) as teens.

Chapter 10

Let's Get Personal

Let me tell y'all a little bit about when Pops got home and his character throughout his life. First things, first. Pops was stalked and tracked by the CIA for decades. Pops said he would pop up at places and there they go. The unmarked cars, the sunglasses, the shirt and tie, white guys. Pops said it happened too many times to be a coincidence. At one point, Pops moved to the Country of Belize just to get away from the CIA. I clearly remember and I know my brother does too. I remember the agents coming to my grandparent's house looking for Pops. White guys in sunglasses. My brother and I were not even in kindergarten yet; 2 and 3 or 3 and 4 years old and I know we both remember it clearly. My mom or grandmother would simply say he wasn't there, and they hadn't seen him since the War. Eventually, when Pops called months later, she would tell him they're looking for you. The family naturally assumed Pops had done something on the Black Power side, maybe trying to start a revolution or something along that line. It was my research that uncovered the Mac-V SOG Team and Pops' involvement with the CIA in Vietnam and Laos. The CIA was looking for Pops because he went AWOL on them and their secret illegal SOG team. Pops was listed as MIA for 6 months, then to pop up in America. Yes, the CIA had questions and maybe charges for Pops. So, Pops lived low-key under the radar for decades. As for my mom, when Pops got home, they tried, but it didn't work. Pops was too different now. Too radical. Mom chose the kids and a regular life over Sylvester and his new radical style.

My mom and Pops got married when he came home for

Vietnam. It lasted 2 years until they separated. This was when Pops had us marching in circles, singing marine anthem, at 1 and 2 years old. Pops did not live with me and my brother again until I was 21 years old. All in between there, Pops would just pop up at different times and every time he popped up, it was like the Hero was Here. War Story Time. Pops telling us those stories were some of his proudest moments in his life. He loved to look in our eyes and see the effects and hear the questions from him telling kids these amazing war Hero stories.

My Pops was a tough cat and super cool. Here are three examples of tough. All three stories, my bro was right next to me listening or witnessing. So, when me and bro were 12 and 13 years old, we got a call from Big M. That's Grandmother, Pops' mom. She called and told my mom that Pops had been shot on the westside of Chicago. We immediately went to the hospital.

Now remember Pops was never shot in Vietnam, but in Chicago, Pops was shot. Pops as shot in the right shoulder. The bullet traveled through the body and came out of his left waistline. Pops was in critical condition. As me and bro walked in with the Oriental nurse, Pops was unconscious, hooked up to all these machines. You could hear the beep of the heartbeat machine. She wakes Pops saying, "Mr. Bracey, these are your two sons." Pops was fuzzy at first, then he rolled his eyes in body language saying I know and see my sons here. At this point, we knew he was alert. Pops couldn't talk though. Pops had a big tube in his mouth and was hooked up to all these machines. At first glance, it did not look good. Pops had blood caked up and dried all down his arm, hands, and fingers, even under his nails. Pops looked weak like he had lost a lot of blood. Being conscious with his index finger, he wiggled to come closer to the bed and we did. All through telepathy and sign language, we talked. Pops made us follow his eyes to look at his body. He rolled his eyes again, like yeah, I'm kinda messed up! Pops wiggled his finger again and pointed to our pictures in our hands. Mom had us bring class pictures. Pops one by one looked at the pics, looked at us, and gave us a nod of approval. Thirty seconds later, Pops coughed for a second and fell back unconscious as the nurse walked us out of the room. At 12 and 13 years old, this was a devastating scene to witness of course and me and my bro remember vividly seeing our dad shot up and laying there fighting for his life. At 12 and 13 years of age, it was devastating to actually see your dad fighting for his life.

Out of Body Experience

My Pops told us this story weeks after he was out of the hospital. Pops said, "You know they lost me a couple of times. The nurse told me that I was gone for 2 to 3 minutes. DEAD. They had to bring me back to life. Marrk, it's kinda funny, but I had a dream that I died and I pushed my will to live. So, in the dream, it's peaceful, it's all white. It's like my head appears in a cloud in the corner of the room by the ceiling, where a security camera would be. That's me looking at the doctors and nurses working on me in a hospital bed. I'm just watching from the top corner of the room, face in the cloud. One side of me said you are tired; you know you can give up. Another side of me said, wake up, they are talking about you. As I looked again and realized the flat line buzzer had been flat for some time now. I noticed the doctors pumping my chest and saying, we're losing him.... we're losing him. Then, I told myself, Hey Jack. They are talking about you. Then I told myself you better breathe. Breathe. Then, I heard the flatline heartbeat mode stop and go back into a regular beep mode. Beep, Beep, Beep. Then I woke up the next day and they told me, I died on the table, and they brought me back. Marrk, I saw it all just out of my body."

You can imagine that ride home from the hospital was very, very quiet. So, two days later in the morning, we go to the hospital to check on Pops. The hospital staff said, "Your dad checked himself out of the hospital last night. We don't know where your father is." Pops called us a few days later and said he was on the Northside recuperating. Ya know, they can't keep a good man down too long. We finally get to ask Pops what happened? Mom took us to the Northside to see him. As we walked in Pops looked fine, camouflage pants on, no shirt, bandaged up. As we entered, we interrupted Pops shooting at squirrels on the electric lines. Target practice, nevertheless. We asked, what happened? Pops said, "It was like this. I'm the manager at BBQ joint. A guy ordered Tips, 30 minutes before closing and didn't come back until we were closing down and tried to rob the joint. The guy pulled out a gun and asked for the money. The girls started hollering and running around. I did a spin move to the other room and came back with mine, Blasting!! We were shooting. It was bullets ricocheting all over the place. The girls screaming in the background. I waited for a second to get one good shot and when I came around the doorway to shoot, he was pointing right at me. Straight through the so-called bulletproof plexiglass. He hit me in the shoulder, and it went across my body. Next thing I remember, I was waking up in a pool of blood and the police saying, Put the Gun Down. I looked, I slid it to 'em, and I passed back out. The next time I woke up, I saw y'all in the hospital with y'all pictures." Because Pops got shot, Mom was bringing us around Pops much more and Pops was pouring on the war stories of course.

Here was another example of Pops' toughness and then I will give you some examples of Pops' character. This was a Pops and Uncle Stan's moment in the 70's. So, Pops was driving with my uncle, trailing him. They were going to the Roadrunner Restaurant over East by Torrence. Pops got into a road rage thing with another driver. Pops and the other guy pull in and get out arguing as Stan parks on the other side. Stan walks around the building and sees Pops in a froze position and the guy has a gun pointing at Pops. My uncle Stan simply walks up and puts his gun to the guy's head and says, "Drop it or I'll Blow Yo Mfing Brains Out Right Here." He dropped the gun instantly and Pops picked it up as he pulled out his. They smacked him around a little bit and then walked into the

Roadrunner with three pistols instead of 2. This was how we grew up. This was who we learned from. Alpha Males. Yes, my pops and Uncle were tough as nails. My dad is gone. My uncle is still here. Both of them made an imprint on my life. So when you see the Alpha male show up, that's where that comes from.

Now to talk about character and why so many people LOVE my pops. Yes, my pops was the coolest man to walk the Earth. Yes, he also spoke in melodies. Like his quote in the viral video "That's Not My Culture." After the war, Pops lived as a humble Giant. When Pops spoke, it was alluring and magnetic to all. Pops practiced wordplay growing up as he studied the dictionary as a hobby. One of Pops' biggest slogans was "Knowledge is Power." Pops read hundreds of books and could remember all the stories. When it came to world history, Pops was sharp, no studying was needed. He could tell you what happened to Alexander the Great, Napoleon, Genghis Khan, Marcus Anthony, etc. because Pops was a perfectionist. My Pops taught himself how to be an electrician. Some of this knowledge came from the military like being a generator man, armory, making bombs, and defusing bombs too. My mom and pops were artists. They could both draw and paint. I saw my pops paint a whole room without dropping one drip of paint. No drop cloth was needed.

My Pops read tarot cards, read palms, studied, and followed Universal Laws, not man-made laws. We would go to a local grocery store. Pops gets to talking, next thing I know he's saying, "Let me see your hand?" It was over. They wouldn't let Pops go as the crowd grew for people wanting their palms read. That was everywhere, every day. Pops was a celebrity amongst the small people everywhere we went. Pops attracted all, even people he disagreed with. If you watch his videos on YouTube, you will see his charm, it's natural. In Pops' eyes, every person has a voice and natural right. Pops was fair and gave everybody a chance. Pops believed in No Big I and Lil You. We are all the same. Let me wrap this up because I could go on and on.

Finally, in closing, I hope that you were entertained. I hope that you learned some things. I hope that in his spirit, your AWOL moment whatever it was, that you choose to do what's best for your survival, not what they tell you. Your Survival. On that note, I would like to thank you for your time, energy and reception. I hope you enjoyed the book.

Special Note: *To Sylvester Bracey, III and Cameron Bracey. While Pops was in Hospice in 2019, Pops said verbatim, Marrk one of my biggest regrets in life was not spending more time with them boys. You know, my grandsons. I wanted to tell them the stories the same way I did you and Sly Baby. You know, teach 'em about the War, teach 'em about life. I know you know more of the stories, and I don't know if your brother's gonna tell 'em. Make sure they know my stories, so they will know what they are made of.*

I gotcha Pops. They will know. Everybody will know when I write the book. Pops replied, "My Man. My Man."

Pops taught me the Spirit Never Dies. So, He's Right Here With Us In Spirit.

Thank you Pops.

I Love You.

Never To be Forgotten!

Bracey Camp

If you want to hear and see my dad speaking live in Vietnam War, go to YouTube and look up Sylvester Bracey, Sr. Marine Vietnam Racism and Discrimination in Vietnam 1970. Several of his videos will pop up. NOW YOU KNOW who you just read about. I hope you learned something and enjoyed the stories. Hopefully, my next project will be Thru His Eyes, the movie.

THRU HIS EYES

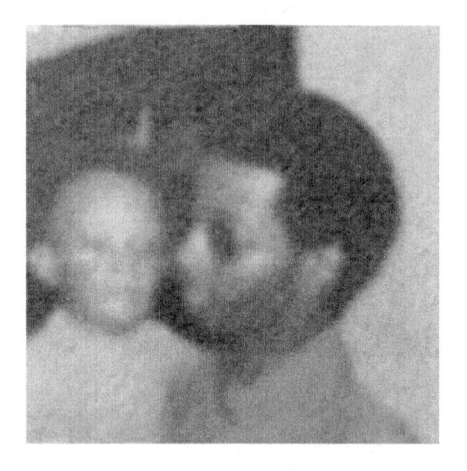

Sylvester Bracey, Sr. and Markus Bracey

Bracey Men
(From L to R) Markus Bracey, Sylvester Bracey, Sr. and Sylvester Bracey, Jr

Sylvester Bracey, Sr.

3 Generations of Bracey Men
(From L to R) Sylvester Bracey, III; Sylvester Bracey, Jr.; Sylvester Bracey, Sr. and Markus Bracey

REFERENCES

African Diaspora News Channel (July 24, 2020). *African American Soldiers Discuss The Method WS Used To Make Vietnamese People Dislike Them.* https://youtu.be/A6JLCopmvGw

Collection of the Smithsonian National Museum of African American History and Culture, Gift of Pearl Bowser. (1971). The Black G.I. (Black Journal segment). https://nmaahc.si.edu/object/nmaahc_2012.79.1.51.1a

The BluePrint. (August 7, 2020).*The Untold Stories Of Black Marine Veterans In Asia 1970 (FULL VIDEO).* https://youtu.be/nNExnLhtHlo

Willingham, Jerome (July 26,2020). Black Marines in Vietnam Discrimination. https://youtu.be/nePBP-6UOjl

ABOUT THE AUTHOR

Markus Bracey is the eldest son of Sylvester Bracey Sr. and Angela Allen. He is a proud veteran who followed in his father's footsteps by serving in the army and later the navy as a double-breasted soldier. He currently resides in Chicago, Illinois where he continues to spread the words of his father to the world.

Made in the USA
Middletown, DE
20 September 2021